S. Hrg. 114–76

CYBERSECURITY: SETTING THE RULES FOR RESPONSIBLEGLOBALCYBERBEHAVIOR

HEARING

BEFORE THE

SUBCOMMITTEE ON EAST ASIA, THE PACIFIC, AND INTERNATIONAL CYBERSECURITY POLICY

OF THE

COMMITTEE ON FOREIGN RELATIONS UNITED STATES SENATE

ONE HUNDRED FOURTEENTH CONGRESS

FIRST SESSION

MAY 14, 2015

Printed for the use of the Committee on Foreign Relations

Available via the World Wide Web: http://www.gpo.gov/fdsys/

U.S. GOVERNMENT PUBLISHING OFFICE

96–851 PDF   WASHINGTON : 2015

For sale by the Superintendent of Documents, U.S. Government Publishing Office
Internet: bookstore.gpo.gov   Phone: toll free (866) 512–1800; DC area (202) 512–1800
Fax: (202) 512–2104   Mail: Stop IDCC, Washington, DC 20402–0001

COMMITTEE ON FOREIGN RELATIONS

BOB CORKER, TENNESSE, *Chairman*

JAMES E. RISCH, Idaho
MARCO RUBIO, Florida
RON JOHNSON, Wisconsin
JEFF FLAKE, Arizona
CORY GARDNER, Colorado
DAVID PERDUE, Georgia
JOHNNY ISAKSON, Georgia
RAND PAUL, Kentucky
JOHN BARRASSO, Wyoming

BENJAMIN L. CARDIN, Maryland
BARBARA BOXER, California
ROBERT MENENDEZ, New Jersey
JEANNE SHAHEEN, New Hampshire
CHRISTOPHER A. COONS, Delaware
TOM UDALL, New Mexico
CHRISTOPHER MURPHY, Connecticut
TIM KAINE, Virginia
EDWARD J. MARKEY, Massachusetts

LESTER E. MUNSON III, *Staff Director*
JODI B. HERMAN, *Democratic Staff Director*

SUBCOMMITTEE ON EAST ASIA, THE PACIFIC, AND INTERNATIONAL CYBERSECURITY POLICY

CORY GARDNER, Colorado, *Chairman*

MARCO RUBIO, Florida
RON JOHNSON, Wisconsin
JOHNNY ISAKSON, Georgia
JEFF FLAKE, Arizona

BENJAMIN L. CARDIN, Maryland
BARBARA BOXER, California
CHRISTOPHER A. COONS, Delaware
TOM UDALL, New Mexico

(II)

CONTENTS

CYBERSECURITY: SETTING THE RULES FOR RESPONSIBLE GLOBAL CYBER BEHAVIOR

THURSDAY, MAY 14, 2015

U.S. SENATE,
SUBCOMMITTEE ON EAST ASIA, THE PACIFIC, AND
INTERNATIONAL CYBERSECURITY POLICY,
COMMITTEE ON FOREIGN RELATIONS,
Washington, DC.

The subcommittee met, pursuant to notice, at 10:02 a.m., in room SD–419, Dirksen Senate Office Building, Hon. Cory Gardner (chairman of the subcommittee) presiding.

Present: Senators Gardner and Cardin.

OPENING STATEMENT OF HON. CORY GARDNER, U.S. SENATOR FROM COLORADO

Senator GARDNER. All right, the committee will be in order.

Thank you very much for the opportunity to be here today. And welcome to the first hearing for the Senate Foreign Relations Committee, Subcommittee on East Asia, The Pacific, and International Cybersecurity Policy.

I want to thank Chairman Corker for his cooperation as this committee is starting its important responsibilities here in the 114th Congress. Of course, we have had numerous hearings on matters relating to East Asia—just yesterday, of course, related to China and other issues—but this is the first dedicated subcommittee hearing.

I want to thank Senator Cardin, the distinguished ranking member of not only this subcommittee, but your plate is now fully full with the full committee. So, thank you very much for being here and taking the time to make this a priority of yours, as well.

Today's hearing is timely, for a multitude of reasons. Cybersecurity is a new area of jurisdiction for this committee which reflects the critical importance this issue has come to play in the foreign affairs of our Nation. Facing a host of known and emerging threats in cyberspace that threatens not only our Nation's critical national security infrastructure, but our economic stability and the privacy of our citizens.

The President's 2011 International Strategy for Cyberspace, which serves as the guide for our Nation's policy, lays out the following strategic goal: The United States will work internationally to promote an open interoperable, secure, and reliable information and communications infrastructure that supports international trade in commerce, strengthens international security, and fosters free expression and innovation. To achieve that goal, we will build

(1)

and sustain an environment in which norms of responsible behavior guides states' actions, sustain partnership, and support the rule of law in cyberspace.

Yet, we know that there are state actors in the field—most prominently, Russia, China, North Korea, and Iran—that have conducted cyber activities that are fundamentally at odds with these goals. As the title of our hearing suggests, how successful has United States policy been in building of a reliable international framework to enforce responsible behavior in cyberspace? How assertive is U.S. diplomacy in both deterring these known threats, but also building viable coalitions with our partners around the world that share our vision of open, interoperable, secure, and reliable information and communication infrastructure?

We also know the President has punitive U.S. measures at his disposal, as demonstrated by the sanctions imposed by the U.S. Department of Justice and when it indicted five Chinese military members in May 2014 for malicious cyber activities directed against our Nation.

On April 1, 2015, the President issued Executive Order 13694 that would impose U.S. sanctions on entities that are, ''engaging in significant malicious cyber-enabled activities.'' So, the question is: How effective have these sanctions been to date in deterring bad actors and encouraging responsible cyber behavior?

We also know that the cyber field is rapidly developing. As technology becomes increasingly sophisticated, so does the task of deterring bad actors and promoting good global cyber governance. It is been 4 years since the President's Strategy for International Cyberspace was put forward. As we know, in technology terms, 4 years might as well be four centuries. And is it time to review an update to that strategy?

So, I hope to explore these and other questions today with our distinguished witnesses on both panels. And, with that, of course, I would like to turn to our distinguished ranking member, Senator Cardin, for his comments.

STATEMENT OF HON. BENJAMIN L. CARDIN, U.S. SENATOR FROM MARYLAND

Senator CARDIN. Well, Senator Gardner, first of all, thank you, and congratulations on your position as the Chair of the East Asia and Pacific Subcommittee. I had the honor of chairing the committee in the last Congress, and the jurisdiction of this committee is critically important to our country. And I know it is in good hands. So, I thank you for doing that.

We know about the President's rebalance to Asia and the importance of the Asia region in regards to our economic and security issues. I know this subcommittee is going to be very, very busy. But, to add to your responsibilities, you now have cybersecurity. I know there are a lot of committees that deal with cybersecurity, but, I must tell you, the international impact and our international coordination is critically important to the security of this country. So, this subcommittee has a particularly important function within not just the Senate Foreign Relations Committee, but within the entire United States Senate and Government. So, good luck, and I look forward to working with you. And I know we are going to work together for our country. So, I look forward to that.

We always knew that we had cyber criminals that were out there. It costs industry a lot of money, costs people a lot of money all the time. We also knew that we are at risk of cyber terrorists, people who want to cause harm to our country. And we knew that was an increased risk. But, I think North Korea's cyber attack on Sony Pictures Entertainment last November was a turning point. We now recognize that we are under direct attack by cyber soldiers organized by government to attack our country—that really changes the whole dynamics of cybersecurity. So, it is a critically important field.

Last month, media reported that Russia has increased its cyber attacks against the United States since sanctions were put in place over Russia's intervention in Ukraine—targeting the most senior levels of the United States Government, as well as a number of U.S. companies—in an attempt to regain the upper hand for Russia's industries adversely impacted by international sanctions. And just last Friday, the State Department expressed United States concerns that China has used a new offensive cyber weapon, referred to as "The Great Cannon," to target foreign and Chinese activist Web sites hosting content banned by China. Mainly, this represents a new level of information censorship by the Chinese.

Price Waterhouse Cooper's study, released last October, found that the number of detected cyber attacks—detected cyber attacks—worldwide escalated dramatically in 2014 to approximately 43 million—up 48 percent in 2013—amounting to about 117,000 attacks every day. So, this is a huge problem that we have to deal with. The global nature of cyber threats requires the United States to bring to bear all of our expertise and resources to ensure that we are doing all we can to protect our Nation's strategic, economic, and security interests, as well as those of our international partners and allies. But, we must do so in a way that preserves Internet freedom—so that people across the world have free and unfettered access to the Internet as a medium through which they can learn, connect, and express themselves. We must uphold our values of openness and respect for human rights in an increasingly digitized world.

I commend the Obama administration for releasing the International Strategy for Cyberspace and strengthening the United States Government's capabilities, particularly in terms of organization and expertise. In February of this year, the President directed the Director of National Intelligence to establish the Cyber Threat Intelligence Integration Center, whose mission is to "connect the dots." That is very, very important. We have a lot of information. We do need to connect the dots. And I hope we will have a chance to get an update on that during this hearing as to what is affecting national interests. The President also issued two new cyber-related Executive orders this year.

As the United States moves forward with these initiatives, we must ensure that the wide array of federal departments and agencies involved in cybersecurity avoid duplicating efforts or overlapping in authorities. We must also continue to reevaluate our current diplomatic strategy and government structure to ensure that we are postured to adapt to the new threats.

One area that I believe holds great promise is public-private partnership. In this respect, Maryland is at the center of our Nation's cybersecurity efforts. In Maryland, we have several federal facilities charged with defending U.S. military networks and assisting our combat commanders and soldiers who work in cyberspace. And I have had a chance to visit these agencies. At Fort Meade, the U.S. Cyber Command plans, coordinates, and conducts full spectrum of military cyberspace operations. That is located just a few miles from where we are. And the National Security Agency and the Central Security Service, also colocated at Fort Meade, work to exploit signal intelligence to collect information on our adversaries and protect U.S. military networks from cyber attack.

In Gaithersburg, MD, the National Institute of Standards and Technology has conducted cybersecurity research for decades and leads the government in standards development and protocol for cybersecurity operations, testings, and certifications.

And, Mr. Chairman, I could tell you all about our universities, which are specialized in cybersecurity. I am very happy that Professor Michael Greenberger is here from the University of Maryland's Center of Health and Homeland Security, a professor at University of Maryland Francis King Carey School of Law. I mention that because I am a graduate of that law school, so we will give plugs whenever we can. [Laughter.]

And I am proud of the fact that the State of Maryland and our local governments have all made cybersecurity a top priority for our State. And I will confess that we do that, in part, because it is good for our business, our jobs, our economy. We have a lot of highly trained people that are getting great jobs in our State. But, we are also doing it because we can perform a mission to this country that is critically important, and we are proud of what the people of Maryland are doing, working on behalf of our national security in cybersecurity.

So, Mr. Chairman, as we start this hearing, we know that we have to engage the private sector. The government cannot do this alone. We really have no choice but to work closely with the private sector. And when I was on the Judiciary Committee, I chaired a subcommittee that had jurisdiction over cybersecurity. I introduced legislation that was incorporated in the Commerce Committee legislation that dealt with trying to harmonize how the private sector deals with their cybersecurity needs. We have started down this path, but we need to do more. We have got to work together on this. What concerns me is that there are a lot of cyber attacks out there in the private sector that we never hear about because they are embarrassed to tell us about it, and we need to make sure that we have the protocols in place so we can protect the security of our country. I think that this hearing today and the work of this subcommittee can help us achieve those objectives for the people of this country.

Senator GARDNER. Thank you, Senator Cardin.

We will begin with our first panel and welcome the Honorable Christopher Painter, who serves as the State Department's Coordinator for Cyber Issues. In this capacity, Mr. Painter coordinates and leads the United States diplomatic efforts to implement the President's International Strategy for Cyberspace. He works closely with components across the Department, other agencies, the White House, the private sector, and civil society. Prior to joining the State Department, Mr. Painter served in the White House as Senior Director for Cybersecurity Policy in the National Security Staff. During his 2 years at the White House, Mr. Painter was a senior member of the team that conducted the President's Cyberspace Policy Review and subsequently served as the Acting Cybersecurity Coordinator. He coordinated the development of the President's 2011 International Strategy for Cyberspace which both Senator Cardin and I have already spoken about.

So, welcome, Mr. Painter. Thank you for your service, and look forward to hearing your testimony today.

STATEMENT OF CHRISTOPHER PAINTER, COORDINATOR FOR CYBER ISSUES, U.S. DEPARTMENT OF STATE, WASHINGTON, DC

Mr. PAINTER. Thank you very much, Senator.

Chairman Gardner, Ranking Member Cardin, members of the Senate Foreign Relations Committee's Subcommittee on East Asia, the Pacific, and International Cybersecurity Policy, it is a real pleasure to be here today to speak with you about our cyber foreign policy, particularly as this, as you mentioned, is your first hearing since the subcommittee took on the important international cybersecurity policy portfolio.

On behalf of my office and the State Department, I look forward to working with you. And I should say that, having been involved in this area now for about 24 years, I am very happy—and this really exemplifies how important this has become as a policy issue, as a national security, economic, human rights, and, ultimately, a foreign policy issue.

We live today in an environment of growing threats, both technical and policy related, to the global Internet we seek to preserve and expand. Our work to respond to these threats is guided by the vision of the U.S. International Strategy for Cyberspace, which seeks to promote an Internet that is open, interoperable, secure, and reliable. The State Department works across a range of interconnected cyber policy issues to achieve this vision through our diplomatic efforts. These issues include promoting cyber stability among States through norms and confidence-building measures; building the domestic cybersecurity capacity of our partners and channels for international cooperation on incident response; fighting cyber crime; advancing human rights online; promoting the continuation of an effective multistakeholder model of Internet governance; and working to address Internet access and affordability issues.

Given time constraints, I am going to focus my oral testimony now primarily on a few security concerns, but I am happy to address questions on this full range of cyber issues.

Let me start with our long-term goal. We are striving for a state of international cyber stability, an environment where all states are able to enjoy the benefits of cyber space, where there are benefits for states to cooperate and avoid conflict, and where there is little incentive for states to attack one another. We are pursuing efforts along two lines to achieve this goal.

First, we are working to develop a shared understanding about norms and responsible state behavior in cyberspace. We believe that developing shared norms will enhance stability, ground foreign and defense policies, guide international partnerships, and help prevent the misunderstandings that can lead to conflict. In recent years, we have had tangible success in developing these norms. Notably, a landmark consensus in 2013 that international law applies to state conduct in cyberspace. We are now working to expand this consensus and look more closely exactly how international law applies. In addition, because cyber tools can be used across the spectrum of conflict, most notably below the threshold of the use of force, the U.S. Government has also been working to identify some voluntary norms of responsible state behavior during peacetime that would be universally appropriate and would keep all of us safer if states adopt them. I have included these norms in my written testimony, but I am happy to discuss them further if you have questions.

In addition to promoting norms, we have also worked to establish practical cyber risk-reduction and confidence-building measures among states. WE believe that effective CBMs can reduce the risk of escalation due to misunderstanding or miscalculation regarding a cyber incident. For example, in December 2013, we achieved an agreement at the Organization for Security and Cooperation in Europe for the first-ever cyber CBMs among members of a multinational security organization. We are now working to implement the current CBMs and develop them in other regional organizations, such as the ASEAN Regional Forum.

Alongside these efforts with a shorter term focus, we are working to strengthen the ability of the U.S. Government as well as our foreign partners to respond to cyber events as they occur. We strongly support increased direct international cooperation among computer security incident response teams and law enforcement entities to respond to and investigate cyber incidents, and we use our diplomatic engagements to help our interagency partners at DHS and DOJ build those ties.

Among our foreign partners, we encourage the development of whole-of-government national strategies and cooperation with the private sector on cybersecurity matters. We have placed a major emphasis on providing capacity-building support to countries that need it so that they are better prepared to do their part when an incident occurs. We also stand ready to support whole-of-government responses to cyber events as they occur, supporting interagency deliberations on major cyber events, and engaging diplomatic channels when needed. For example, during the 2012–2013 distributed denial-of-service attacks against our financial institutions, State used diplomatic channels as a supplement to incident response efforts through more technical channels. State also works closely with DOJ colleagues to strengthen international cooperation to combat transnational cyber crime and other forms of high-tech crime. We support the Budapest Convention on Cybercrime, as well as the G7 24/7 network, which allows national police to request rapid assistance in significant investigations involving digital evidence. State also works with our colleagues in DOJ to provide capacity-building assistance on investigation and prosecuting cyber crimes.

I should, finally, note that all of our work to promote security takes place in the context of our broader commitment to an open and interoperable global Internet. That is why states' work on Internet governance, Internet freedom, and promoting ICTs as an engine for development is so closely tied to our work in promoting security.

I am now happy to take any questions.

[The prepared statement of Mr. Painter follows:]

PREPARED STATEMENT OF CHRISTOPHER M.E. PAINTER

Chairman Gardner, Ranking Member Cardin, members of the Senate Foreign Relations Committee Subcommittee on East Asia, the Pacific, and International Cybersecurity Policy, it is a pleasure to be here today to speak about our cyber foreign policy.

Before I begin, I would like to commend your subcommittee for recently taking on "International Cybersecurity Policy" as a part of your portfolio. This development is yet another important step in our government's efforts to strengthen our foreign policy on cyber issues. It is also further recognition of the growing importance of cyber policy to our national security, foreign policy, economy, values, and way of life. Moreover, the fact that cyber policy is the subject of the subcommittee's first hearing during the legislative session indicates the importance you place on this new role. On behalf of my office and the State Department, I look forward to working with you.

CYBER ISSUES: A NEW FOREIGN POLICY IMPERATIVE

When it comes to the foreign policy implications of cyber issues, it is important to begin with the recognition that this subcommittee and the State Department are working in a still-nascent policy space. While the Internet has been growing and evolving for a few decades now, the international community has only more recently begun to fully grasp cyber issues as a foreign policy priority.

Only 4 years ago this month, the White House issued its International Strategy for Cyberspace, leading the world in recognizing the need for a comprehensive and crosscutting strategic approach to this key area. We were also the first country to establish a foreign ministry office like the one I lead—the State Department's Office of the Coordinator for Cyber Issues—to coordinate diplomatic efforts across the full range of international cyber policy issues.

The world has changed dramatically even since then. Now there are offices like ours in foreign ministries throughout the world, and new ones are steadily being created as more countries look to engage in the global cyber policy dialogue. Cyber issues have become central topics of discussion in virtually every international venue, and cyber diplomacy is increasingly viewed by governments as a foreign policy imperative.

Nonetheless, cyber issues remain in many respects an emerging area of foreign and national security policy. The global community is still in an early stage of tackling these challenging issues and building consensus toward solutions that are consistent with the core values of democracy and human rights. In the United States, we have made great strides in articulating our strategic vision for cyberspace, but we are still working to fully develop the necessary capabilities to ensure we can continue to lead in this dynamic policy area and respond to crises as they emerge.

These efforts occur in a context of growing threats—both technical and policy related—to the open and interoperable global Internet we seek to preserve and expand. On the technical side, we face increasing risks from state and nonstate actors that conduct malicious cyber activity for the purpose of stealing trade secrets or personal information for commercial or financial gain, suppressing freedom of expression, destroying data, harming our critical infrastructure, or causing various other types of harm. North Korea's cyber attack on Sony Pictures Entertainment demonstrated the potential coercive effects of such activity. The more recent targeting of Github highlights a new and worrying trend of cyber capabilities being used from abroad to influence public expression within the United States. While, as the Director of National Intelligence recently noted, the "likelihood of a catastrophic attack from any particular actor is remote at this time," we are likely to see "an ongoing series of low-to-moderate level cyber attacks from a variety of sources'' that will, over time, ''impose costs on U.S. economic competitiveness and national security.''

In the policy context, we face significant and growing challenges, especially from China, Russia, and other authoritarian governments that seek increased sovereign control over the Internet and its content. These challenges surface in a variety of fora and across a range of policy issues. Internet governance is a prime example of a challenging cyber policy area. Here, we see governments that are more concerned with regime stability than with economic and social development pushing to shift from the long-standing and successful multistakeholder model—one that involves active participation by governments, the private sector, civil society, and academia in an inclusive and bottom-up process—to an intergovernmental and exclusive system that could fundamentally undermine the future growth and potential of the Internet. The fight against transnational cyber crime is another area where we face a policy challenge. China and Russia are aggressively advocating for a new global cyber-crime agreement that would serve as a vehicle for controlling speech and undermining civil and political rights, while at the same time criticizing the effectiveness of existing international instruments like the Council of Europe Convention on Cybercrime, or Budapest Convention.

Our work to respond to these threats is guided by the vision of the U.S. International Strategy for Cyberspace, which seeks ''to promote an open, interoperable, secure, and reliable information and communications infrastructure that supports international trade and commerce, strengthens international security, and fosters free expression and innovation.'' The State Department—not just my office, but the full complement of security, economic, human rights, law enforcement and regionally focused bureaus and offices throughout the Department—works across a range of interconnected cyber policy issues to achieve this vision through our diplomatic efforts. This includes promoting cyber stability among states through norms and confidence building measures, building the domestic cyber security capacity of our partners and channels for international cooperation on incident response, fighting cyber crime, advancing human rights online, promoting the continuation of an effective multistakeholder model of Internet governance, and, in cooperation with our colleagues at USAID among others, promoting capacity building, technical assistance, and development programs to tackle security challenges and address Internet access and affordability issues.

Accordingly, my office works closely with offices and officials across the Department—including Under Secretary for Economic Growth, Energy, and the Environment, Catherine Novelli, who serves as the Senior Coordinator for International Information Technology Diplomacy; the Bureau of Democracy, Human Rights and Labor; the Bureau of International Narcotics and Law Enforcement; the Bureau of Economics and Business Affairs Office of International Communications and Information Policy; the Bureau of Counterterrorism; the Bureau of Arms Control and Verification; among other functional components, and every regional bureau. We also coordinate our work with colleagues throughout the Federal Government, including at the Departments of Defense, Justice, Homeland Security, Commerce, and Treasury.

The State Department is a key player in all U.S. Government interagency cyber policy processes, ensuring that timely and pertinent foreign policy guidance is provided to decision makers at all levels. Given the global nature of the Internet, even ostensibly domestic cyber policy decisions typically have a foreign policy or diplomatic dimension. We also leverage State's global diplomatic corps, including our growing cadre of cyber officers, to support the vision articulated in the U.S. International Strategy for Cyberspace, and respond to growing threats.

REVIEW OF THE GLOBAL CYBER LANDSCAPE

Before describing our international priorities in detail, it is useful to review some of the most recent cyber developments from around the world to better frame the kinds of challenges and opportunities that we face. We can call it a short ''cyber policy world tour.''

Given the subcommittee's focus on East Asia and the Pacific, I will begin there. As you know, this dynamic region is playing an increasingly important role in the world, particularly in the area of cyber policy. Within the region, there is much focus on China's role in cyberspace. In recent years, China has become more assertive in promoting its vision for cyberspace—government-controlled, with an absolutist conception of sovereignty over technology and content—that stands in stark contrast to our own policy priorities. As we push back against these repressive concepts, we also continue to engage China on areas of potential cooperation, such as network defense and other practical measures that could reduce the risk of conflict in cyberspace. At the same time, the administration has been clear, consistent, and direct in raising our concerns with the Chinese regarding issues such as state-sponsored cyber-enabled theft of intellectual property for commercial gain. We have also been concerned by recent reports that China has used a new cyber capability to interfere with the ability of worldwide Internet users to access content hosted outside of China, including the web developer site Github. Although we regret China's decision to suspend the activities of the U.S.-China Cyber Working Group, we have continued to engage Chinese cyber experts on areas of concern. We remain committed to expanding our cooperation with the Chinese Government on cyber matters where we have common ground and to candidly and constructively addressing differences.

The United States maintains strong and ongoing diplomatic relations on cyber issues with a number of other countries in the region. We work very closely across the range of cyber policy topics with our friends in Japan, South Korea, Australia, and New Zealand, with whom we share a common vision for cyberspace. During Prime Minister Shinzo Abe's visit to Washington in April 2015, both the United States and Japan reaffirmed their commitment to working together "to ensure the safe and stable use of cyberspace based on the free flow of information and an open Internet." The United States also engages on regional security issues in the ASEAN Regional Forum, where we are actively promoting the development of regional cyber confidence-building measures. We are seeking to expand our bilateral engagement with several ASEAN states, including Indonesia, Singapore, and Malaysia, and actively promoting cyber crime capacity-building efforts in the region in partnership with Japan and Australia.

Finally, the region includes North Korea, which was responsible for the November 2014 cyber attack on Sony Pictures Entertainment. The destructiveness of that cyber attack, coupled with its coercive nature, sets it apart from other malicious cyber activity we have observed in recent years. This is why the President publicly attributed the cyber attack to North Korea and vowed that we would "respond proportionally . . . in a place and time and manner that we choose." In January 2015, the President signed a new Executive order, increasing our ability to apply sanctions pressure in response to the provocative, destabilizing, and repressive actions and policies of the Government of North Korea, such as the destructive and coercive Sony Pictures cyber attack.

Next, we can turn to Europe, which largely shares our vision for an open and secure Internet, but which still contains security and policy challenges. The United States has very close relations with much of Europe and our cooperation in the region on cyber issues is increasing. We engage directly with the European institutions on cyber, notably the European External Action Service (EAS). Working with the EAS, we have launched a U.S.-EU Cyber Dialogue to address the cyber foreign policy matters of mutual concern and align our foreign policy posture on key issues in international fora.

My office leads regular bilateral engagements on cyber policy with individual countries like the United Kingdom, Germany, and France and has built regional collaborative engagements with the Nordic and Baltic countries, including a cyber partnership statement with Estonia. We have emerging engagements, including increased outreach from our embassies, with Spain, Portugal, and Italy, among others, as they have increasingly joined in global cyber policy discussions. Our bilateral engagements with some countries, primarily Germany, have been punctuated by continued reactions to unauthorized disclosures and allegations of NSA electronic surveillance activities. We continue to work closely with the administration and our colleagues within the Department to address the concerns we hear from our foreign partners.

While Eastern Europe has traditionally been the source—or conduit—for significant online criminal activity, there are numerous efforts underway at our embassies, and through other channels, to help build constructive engagement with a number of countries. This includes utilizing resources such as the International Visitor Leadership Program on one hand, and law enforcement capacity-building and liaison programs on the other. As a result, we are starting to see some positive changes in national attitudes, most notably in Ukraine.

Russia is obviously an important cyber actor on the international stage, where it continues to assert its repressive agenda on a wide range of cyber issues. We are closely watching and working to counter their efforts to impose greater state control over the Internet and undermine security and human rights online. Given Russia's ongoing violation of Ukraine's sovereignty and territorial integrity, the United States has suspended our bilateral cyber dialogue with Russia. Nevertheless, we continue to interact with Russia on multilateral efforts in the United Nations and the Organization for Security and Cooperation in Europe (OSCE) to build greater stability and reduce the risk of conflict among states in cyberspace, through the development of norms of responsible state behavior and cyber confidence-building measures. As long as Russia advocates an antidemocratic world view on cyber policy issues, we must work with our international partners to counter its destabilizing policies and activities.

The Middle East is a complex place, and we can see cyber issues becoming an increasingly important feature of the already multifaceted security and human rights challenges facing the region. There are real dangers of malicious cyber activity becoming enmeshed within—and potentially escalating—existing regional rivalries, and we have seen groups like ISIL harness the Internet as a tool for terrorist purposes. To guard against these threats, we are committed to working with our international partners in the region, including Israel and the Gulf States, to build a shared understanding of the threat, develop effective strategies and policy, and shore up vulnerabilities, especially in critical infrastructure. Through all of our efforts, we will help protect key U.S. interests and promote regional stability. Of course, promoting cybersecurity cannot come at the expense of the open Internet, which provides a tremendous set of opportunities for economic growth in a region that will be key to long-term development and stability.

South and Central Asia is a region where, despite challenges in some countries, we see new opportunities for engagement and growth. India is pursuing an exciting ''Digital India'' agenda and is making progress on developing its cybersecurity capabilities. Its dynamic civil society, private industry, and technology sectors are increasingly playing leadership roles in cyber policy issues, such as Internet governance. With our shared democratic values, robust economic relationship, and people-to-people ties, the United States is primed for close strategic cooperation with India on the full range of cyber issues, and we are eager to strengthen our engagement. When Prime Minister Modi visited the United States in September 2014, we agreed to develop closer cybersecurity cooperation and to reinitiate our whole-of-government Cyber Consultations, which we look forward to pursuing this summer. We are also seeing leadership on cyber issues elsewhere in the region—for instance, Sri Lanka is taking important steps toward becoming the first state in the region to join the Budapest Convention, which will enable it to be a strong partner in combating global cyber crime. Other states are still figuring out how to grapple with cybersecurity and cyber crime challenges, but they are increasingly aware of the economic opportunities an open and interoperable Internet brings and increasingly paying attention.

Closer to home, within the Western Hemisphere we are presented with numerous opportunities to build stronger partnerships on the range of cyber issues, working bilaterally, within regional bodies like the Organization of American States (OAS), with civil society and with the private sector. The United States has had long-standing relationships with important actors in this region, including Canada with which we have a shared perspective on cyber policy. Brazil is another important actor on cyber policy, and I colead a bilateral whole-of-government working group with the Brazilians on Internet and ICT policy. As more people within the region gain reliable access to the Internet, more governments are recognizing the need to develop a coordinated strategic approach to cyber policy. With support from the United States and other partners in the region, the OAS has successfully trained law enforcement, judicial experts, and policymakers on the importance of increasing cybersecurity and combating cyber crime. We believe that the OAS work, along with our long-standing efforts to engage bilaterally in the hemisphere, have contributed to the fact that nine Latin American countries are now in various stages of joining the Budapest Convention. Countries like Jamaica, Colombia, Costa Rica, and Chile are making a concerted effort to consult across ministries and to include experts from a variety of local sectors as they develop new legislation, update digital agendas, and craft cybersecurity strategies. Countries like Argentina and Uruguay are honing the skills of their workforce and working to expand their community of cyber experts from urban centers to rural areas. Taken as a whole, our friends in the region are working toward a truly cyber-savvy citizenry, and we are supporting that growth by strengthening existing partnerships and seeking new opportunities for engagement.

The final region on our tour, but certainly not last in our list of priorities, is Africa, a region with relatively low but fast-growing Internet penetration and a strong incentive to build an open, secure, and interoperable Internet as an engine for economic growth. As the use of the Internet and mobile phones expands throughout sub-Saharan Africa, nations are faced with a corresponding increase in the number of cyber threats. Vulnerable networks erode the development benefits of ICTs and pose economic and security challenges to individuals, nations, and the international community. Yet this same technology is contributing to stronger democratic institutions, boosting broad-based economic growth through trade and investment, advancing peace and prosperity, and promoting opportunity and development. This is why African nations have been a significant focus of my office's Foreign Assistance programming. We are working with African leaders and citizens in an enduring, multifaceted partnership on cyber issues—one that is not about overnight solutions or one-off deals, but instead focuses on long-term collaborative efforts among all stakeholders. We are bringing key partners together bilaterally, while working multilaterally with the African Union Commission (AUC) and key Regional Economic Communities to help our partners build and shape effective and sustainable cyber architecture that serves Africa on a regional and global scale. This includes continuing our tradition of training and engagement on cybersecurity best practices, building the requisite legal frameworks for states and individuals to combat the threat of cyber crime, working to maintain open and unfettered access for all Africans, and encouraging African voices and perspectives in the very relevant conversation we are having on how states should work together to prevent cyber conflict. These were the topics of utmost interest to African officials I met in June 2014 when I joined colleagues from across the Southern African Development Community for a 4-day cyber policy training session—the fourth regional workshop in a series that we have presented across the continent—and they will continue to be the focus of our work on the continent in 2015.

Lastly, our cyber world tour would not be complete without discussing the cyber policy debates that are currently taking place in multilateral venues. Here the picture is complicated by the fact that there is a multitude of fora that address the range of cyber issues. For our work in promoting international security and stability in cyberspace, we look to the United Nations and within regional security organizations like the OSCE and the ASEAN Regional Forum. Issues around cyber crime are dealt with in fora like the Council of Europe and the United Nations Office of Drugs and Crime (UNODC). However, cyber issues do not only arise in traditional international fora. Dynamic and decentralized multistakeholder venues that include representation from the private sector and civil society as well as states play a key role in Internet governance, and we work with this range of stakeholders to promote our vision for the Internet.

It is within multilateral venues that we most frequently encounter the types of policy threats that I noted earlier. Countries like Russia and China use these venues to press for greater government control over the Internet, for example, by advocating that the International Telecommunication Union take a greater role in Internet governance and pushing for a United Nations cyber treaty. To date, the United States has worked very effectively with likeminded countries to stave off the challenges in these venues. At the same time, there have been a number of successes in multilateral fora, particularly on security issues, as discussed below.

CYBER POLICY PRIORITIES

This is the world that we face. I am optimistic about our ability to respond to the threats, build cyber stability and resilience, and ultimately continue to capitalize on the rich economic and expressive opportunities that the Internet offers us. But there is much work to be done. I want to spend some time now talking about what the State Department is doing to support whole-of-government efforts to engage the world that we have just toured on cyber policy issues.

1. Security and Cyber Crime

With respect to security issues, our long-term vision is to strive for a state of "international cyber stability": a more peaceful environment where all states are able to enjoy the benefits of cyberspace; where there are benefits to state-to-state cooperation and avoiding conflict; and where there is little incentive for states to attack one another. We are pursuing efforts along two lines to achieve this longer term goal.

First, we are working to develop a shared understanding about norms of responsible state behavior in cyberspace, which will help enhance stability, ground foreign and defense policies, guide international partnerships, and help prevent the misunderstandings that can lead to conflict. In recent years, we have had tangible successes in developing these norms. The 2013 U.N. Group of Governmental Experts on Developments in the Field of Information and Telecommunications in the Context of International Security (GGE)—a group of 15 countries that included the United States as well as countries like Russia and China—reached a landmark consensus that international law applies to state conduct in cyberspace. In the current round of the GGE, we are working to build on this important consensus with an even broader group and look more closely at how international law applies to state conduct in cyberspace.

As part of these efforts, the United States has also been considering what voluntary measures of self-restraint states should implement, since cyber tools can be used across the spectrum of conflict, most notably below the threshold of the use of force. Accordingly we have sought to identify some voluntary norms of responsible state behavior during peacetime that would be universally appropriate and that will keep all of us safer if states adopt them. They include:

- A State should not conduct or knowingly support online activity that intentionally damages critical infrastructure or otherwise impairs the use of critical infrastructure to provide services to the public.
- A State should not conduct or knowingly support activity intended to prevent national CSIRTs from responding to cyber incidents. A State should also not use CSIRTs to enable online activity that is intended to do harm.
- A State should cooperate, in a manner consistent with its domestic law and international obligations, with requests for assistance from other States in investigating cyber crimes, collecting electronic evidence, and mitigating malicious cyber activity emanating from its territory. States must take robust and co-operative action to investigate criminal activity by nonState actors.
- A State should not conduct or knowingly support cyber-enabled theft of intellectual property, including trade secrets or other confidential business information, with the intent of providing competitive advantages to its companies or commercial sectors.

These voluntary measures are beginning to gain traction internationally. During the current round of the GGE, we proposed the inclusion of several of these norms in the group's draft report and many states have spoken positively about their inclusion. In addition, on the occasion of Prime Minister Abe's recent visit to Washington, Japan, and the United States released a leaders-level statement that affirmed that states should uphold additional, voluntary norms of state behavior in cyberspace during peacetime, noting that wide affirmation among states would contribute to international stability in cyberspace. Australia's Foreign Minister also affirmed some of these concepts in recent remarks.

Second, in addition to promoting norms, our international security work has also focused on the establishment of practical cyber risk-reduction and confidence-building measures (CBMs), which are intended to reduce the risk of escalation due to misunderstanding or miscalculation regarding a cyber incident of national security concern emanating from U.S. or another country's territory. The first ever bilateral cyber CBMs were announced by President Obama and President Putin in June 2013. And in December 2013, at the ministerial of the OSCE, we achieved an agreement among the 57 participating states for the first ever cyber CBMs for a multinational security organization. We are now working to implement the current CBMs, and we are also pursuing the development of cyber CBMs in other regional organizations, such as the ASEAN Regional Forum.

Alongside these efforts, and with a shorter term focus, we are working to strengthen the ability of the U.S. Government as well as our foreign partners to respond to cyber events as they occur. We strongly favor increased direct international cooperation among Computer Security Incident Response Teams (CSIRTs) and law enforcement entities to respond to and investigate cyber incidents, and we use our diplomatic engagements to support the building of those ties. Among our foreign partners, we encourage the development of whole-of-government national strategies as well as cooperation with the private sector on cybersecurity matters.

When incidents occur, we stand ready to support the whole-of-government response. State, as the lead foreign policy agency, plays a key role in interagency deliberations on major cyber events, and it engages diplomatic channels where needed. For example, during the 2012–2013 distributed denial of service attacks against financial institutions, State used diplomatic channels as a supplement to incident response efforts through more technical channels, ensuring that policymakers in foreign governments were aware of U.S. requests for assistance. More recently, in response to the cyber attack on Sony Pictures Entertainment, we were pleased to see a number of foreign partners come to our support in condemning North Korea's actions. We have also used diplomatic channels to raise concerns regarding the cyber-enabled theft of trade secrets for commercial gain.

Beyond these efforts, State has supported the administration's ongoing efforts to fully develop its toolkit for deterring and responding to cyber threats. For example, we participated in the development and release of the recently announced Executive Order 13694, which allows for the targeted imposition of financial sanctions against persons engaging in certain significant malicious cyber-enabled activities that are reasonably likely to result in, or have materially contributed to, a significant threat to the national security, foreign policy, or economic health or financial stability of the United States.

State also works closely with Department of Justice colleagues to strengthen international cooperation to combat transnational cyber crime and other forms of high-tech crime. The continued expansion of the Budapest Cybercrime Convention—which has 45 parties representing the Americas, Europe, Asia, the Pacific, and Africa, and more than a dozen additional countries in the final stages of joining—demonstrates the growing realization by governments around the world that cyber crime must be tackled head on, using a consistent and proven legal framework, in order to eliminate criminal safe-havens. Another key tool in our arsenal to counter high-tech crime is the G7 24/7 Network which allows the national police in 70 countries to request rapid assistance in significant investigations involving digital evidence. The State Department is committed to working with like-minded partners around the globe to build both the will and capacity to effectively counter cyber crime, and we will continue to devote significant resources to that goal.

2. Internet Governance and Internet Freedom

We have also seen some recent successes in the areas of Internet governance and promoting human rights online, and we continue to take those efforts forward. In 2014, our work to maintain the current multistakeholder system was bolstered by the U.S. Government announcement of the intent to transfer key Internet domain name functions to the global multistakeholder community; the strong, multistakeholder, consensus-based outcome of the NETmundial conference in Brazil; and the successful completion of the ITU Plenipotentiary Conference in Busan, South Korea, where, with the leadership of my colleague, Ambassador Daniel Sepulveda, we achieved a consensus that avoided expanding or establishing any new mandates for the ITU related to Internet governance or cybersecurity.

This year, we are looking forward to the 10th annual Internet Governance Forum, which will take place in Brazil. The IGF continues to provide a venue for global, multistakeholder dialogue on Internet policy issues that alleviates the need for a more centralized, intergovernmental approach to decisions about how the Internet works and the policies surrounding it. A decision about whether to extend the IGF's mandate will be taken later this year by the U.N. General Assembly as part of their 10-Year Review of the World Summit on the Information Society—the so called WSIS+10 review. The focus of this year's review will be on the growth of the Information Society, essentially ICTs for development, over the last 10 years. We believe there has been tremendous progress, as shown by the exceptional growth of the Internet around the world. Nonetheless, going forward, we will focus our attention and collective efforts on practical measures to close the remaining gaps in access and capacity.

The United States can also count successes in our efforts to promote Internet freedom and human rights online, thanks in large part to the efforts of State's Bureau of Democracy, Human Rights, and Labor (DRL). At the core of our policy approach is the maxim that the same human rights that people have offline also apply online—a view that was adopted by the U.N. Human Rights Council in a 2012 resolution and reaffirmed again in 2014—and this position is mainstreamed across all of State's work, including our efforts to promote cybersecurity and fight cyber crime. Together with my colleague Tom Malinowski, Assistant Secretary of State for DRL, I have just returned from this year's meeting in Ulaanbaatar, Mongolia, of the Freedom Online Coalition, a group of now 26 governments committed to taking concrete action in support of Internet freedom. Programmatically, DRL works with USAID, our Near East Asia bureau and others, to support advocates who promote freedom online, as well as the development of technologies that assist in those efforts.

3. Bilateral Engagements

State's cyber diplomacy also focuses specifically on our bilateral relationships with a number of key countries. Bilateral engagements, or engagements with smaller groupings of countries, provide a valuable opportunity to share views with partners, identify areas of agreement, address differences of opinion, and develop areas for cooperation.

State has pioneered a whole-of-government model for conducting bilateral engagements on cyber policy issues, which brings together cyber policy experts from across our government (for example, from DOD, Justice, DHS, and Commerce) to engage simultaneously with foreign government counterparts. We find that this approach helps avoid uncoordinated discussions between individual agencies on certain topics and at times has the added benefit of encouraging interagency cooperation among our partners.

We are currently conducting formal whole-of-government cyber dialogues with Germany, the Republic of Korea, Japan, the European Union, and the eight Nordic-Baltic States, and we are in the process of reinvigorating dialogues with Brazil and India. As mentioned earlier, we also have official dialogues with China and Russia, both of which are presently suspended. We also regularly engage with Australia, Canada, New Zealand, and the United Kingdom in both formal and informal settings, consistent with our close relationship across the spectrum of security issues. In addition, the State Department conducts less formal cyber bilateral engagements with a number of countries and multilateral organizations. Finally, it should be noted that there are a number of other State policy dialogues that complement our efforts, such as the ICT policy dialogues that Ambassador Sepulveda's office in the Bureau of Economic and Business Affairs leads with key economic partners as well as the human rights dialogues led by DRL.

4. Capacity Building

The State Department and USAID are actively working to build the capacity of foreign governments across a range of interconnected cyber policy issues—with a principal focus on expanding Internet access through innovation, improving domestic cybersecurity through the development of CSIRTs and national strategies, improving the ability to fight cyber crime and other forms of high-tech crime, and ensuring the ability to cooperate with global partners to address shared threats. Recently, the United States became a founding member of the Global Forum for Cyber Expertise, which was launched on April 16, 2015, during the Dutch-hosted Global Conference on Cyberspace in The Hague, reaffirming our commitment to cyber capacity-building.

In particular, recognizing that our ability to fight transnational cyber crime and respond to foreign cyber threats is greatly impacted by the strength of our international partners, State, including our Bureau for International Narcotics and Law Enforcement Affairs, is working with colleagues at the Departments of Justice and Homeland Security to build the capacity of foreign governments to secure their own networks as well as investigate and prosecute cyber criminals within their borders. Working with multilateral organizations like the AUC, the UNODC (via its Global Cybercrime Capacity Building Program), the Council of Europe, the European Union, the G7, and the OAS, we promote cyber crime policies in line with the Budapest Convention and share cybersecurity best practices, such as writing national cyber strategies, forming cybersecurity incident response teams, and promoting public awareness campaigns on good cybersecurity practice. Most recently, at the end of fiscal year 2014, my office obligated over $1 million of our limited foreign assistance funds to Carnegie Mellon University's Software Engineering Institute, a federally funded research and development center, to begin a project in sub-Saharan Africa on cybersecurity incident response and incident management capabilities and coordination. We are hopeful that this and related efforts can expand and serve as a model for future capacity-building assistance programs.

We believe that cyber crime and cybersecurity capacity-building overall must be a priority for the U.S. Government going forward. If they are not adequately addressed by the United States and key partners, then we run the risk that as the Internet continues to expand in the developing world, it will do so without necessary cybersecurity safeguards, creating global risks and undermining the conditions necessary to realize the economic and social benefits offered by expanded broadband access.

5. Mainstreaming Cyber Policy at State

Last, we are working to mainstream cyber policy issues across State and USAID, so that we can more effectively leverage both personnel and budget resources as tools for implementing our cyber policies. Nearly every bureau within the Department—whether regional or functional—now plays some role in cyber policymaking. To prioritize our engagements and resources, we have worked with our regional bureaus to develop cyber-specific regional strategies focusing on key partners in each part of the world. To better leverage our embassies in implementing these regional strategies, we have brought 163 State Foreign Service officers and USAID employees from 121 missions together with U.S. Government experts through an innovative new training program created by my office to train diplomatic officers and support them in their own local cyber engagements. To identify resources and needs, we worked to incorporate cyber priorities into Department budget planning efforts. While this line of work does not involve actual engagement with foreign partners, it is an important part of building our government's capabilities to advance cyber policy issues going forward.

CONCLUSION

Thank you for the opportunity to provide State's perspective on global cyber issues and on our international cyber priorities. We look forward to working with the subcommittee toward protecting our security here at home and ensuring that all of us can continue to benefit from an open, interoperable, secure, and reliable global Internet.

Senator GARDNER. And thank you for your comments.

And I think we have plenty of time to go back and forth in the question period. So, I will go ahead and start with my questions, Mr. Painter. And I thank you, again.

So, I just want to walk through a hypothetical scenario for what your actions would be, and the U.S. diplomatic response to a hypothetical—again, hypothetical—cyber attack. Let us say your office receives notification that our Nation's sensitive cyber networks have been penetrated, and you determine that the attack originated from the great political-science-founded nation of Ruritania. We also know that this nation has been hostile to U.S. interests in the past, and its leadership has prioritized advancing its cyber capabilities to counter U.S. interests. Basically, walk us through. I mean, what are your steps? How does the escalation work, if there is any, across State Department? How do you work with other U.S. Government agencies? And then, what would be your diplomatic response put in place?

Mr. PAINTER. Thank you, Senator.

Let me first start in the larger frame. We are a key part of the interagency process to respond to cyber attacks and cyber intrusions. We work with our interagency to support both the whole-of-government responses, what the law enforcement and technical community would do, and also what the White House and other parts of our government would do, including our Department of Defense. And we build those bridges over time. I would say that one thing I have seen that is a marked difference over the last 5 or 6 years is the amount of coordination among Federal agencies is far better than it has ever been before.

On this particular hypothetical, there would be a couple of things that we would do. First, we would be part of something called the Cyber Response Group, which is a group led by the White House, but it has all the key agencies in it. And we would be discussing this, likely, what the actual facts were, with the technical agencies and the other agencies, to find out what the ground truth is and also to determine how the State Department could contribute its core expertise, which is its diplomatic expertise or also, sometimes, its expertise with partnerships around the world.

Now, stepping back, this really—you know, we have done a lot of prep work before you even get to this point. One thing we would do, and one thing we have done over the last 4 years, is build partnerships with a number of countries around the world. So, it used to be, when my office was started, we were the first office in the Foreign Ministry that did this. Now there are over 20 offices around the world, so I have policy counterparts that I can very quickly get in touch with if we have a cyber incident like this.

But, we supplement that with our other work with our other agencies. And we are also part of what is called the National

Cyberincident Response Plan that is led by DHS but also looks at these issues.

So, if this came up, we would—there are a number of things we could do. We would participate in these interagency discussions. We would look at all the tools that we had as an interagency—law enforcement tools, technical tools, tools like sanctions, for instance. We would have a range of tools, and we are trying to develop new ones. And then we would see how our diplomatic tools could play into that.

So, to give you a couple of quick examples, based on the real world, that I think are helpful, when we had—and I mentioned this in my testimony—we had the denial-of-service attack back in 2012–2013. These were botnets. These were compromised computers all over the world. And so, they were in countries all over the world, and they can shift from day to day. Our technical people were reaching out to all those countries, trying to mitigate that threat. What we did, as the State Department, is, we reached out to—using demarches, diplomatic demarches—to governments, over 20, around the world, which raised the level of concern. It was not just the normal technical request that the Federal Government often makes. We said, ''This is really important to us, and we are trying to build this collection—this collective action against shared threats.'' And we got a lot of assistance from governments, because they understood it was not just a technical issue, it was more of a policy issue, and it was elevated in their governments.

Another good example is during the North Korea Sony attack that was mentioned by Senator Cardin. Again, there was a number of responses to that, and we participated in looking at those responses. But, part of what we did is, when it was clear what the attribution was, and that the President was going to make this attribution, I reached out to counterparts in a number of countries around the world. And a number of those countries condemned the action. And that also shows that that kind of activity is unacceptable—it is a norm that is unacceptable. So, there are a number of things we can do, both using our direct outreach with counterparts and sometimes we will have relationships with governments that other agencies do not have. Many countries now have CERTs, or C–CERTs. Some countries do not, so maybe we can draw those connections. But, we do it as part of a team.

Senator GARDNER. Thank you. And you talk about the demarches and you talk about some of the other actions taken against some of the actors responsible for a cyber attack—suspected cyber, I guess, threat or vandalism, however it is classified. When we are talking about our Foreign Service officers, we are talking about our Ambassadors and work that we are doing around the globe. If you look at the U.S. Army, for instance, they realized that they had certain threats that they needed to recognize at a higher responsibility. The veterinarian—the Veterinary Corps—Veterinarian Corps of the U.S. Army went from being a colonel that they elevated to the rank of general because they believed it was something they needed to pay more attention as the threat of anthrax and other attacks were exposed here in the United States. Do we need to raise the level of concern, raise the level of responsibility, raise the level of priority through our Foreign Service officers in a similar manner?

Mr. PAINTER. So, I actually think we have anticipated that. One of the things when my office was founded—and I think it showed a lot of vision, in saying this really is a priority issue. And having an office like this in the Secretary's office, reporting to the Secretary, indicated that. But, what we then set about doing is making sure that we had cyber-trained officers in all of our relevant posts around the world. We also worked with each—and this is part of the mainstreaming of this issue at the State Department. So, this is a new issue. It is a technical issue, as both of you know. Many people view as a technical issue. I view it as much more than a technical issue, and people now understand that.

But, one of the key things we have done is say, How can we mainstream this issue so it is not just important to us, but important across the State Department and, indeed, across the Government? So, we have done that by having each of our regional bureaus do specific regional cyber strategies across all these buckets I talked about earlier, including the security buckets. We have then taken those regional strategies and we have done training for these post officers in the field, where—we have just completed the last one of these—where we brought, regionally, all the officers in, we had private-sector people, we had other interagency people from DHS and DOJ and DOD come in, and we really tried to bring them up to speed. So, we are, indeed, trying to raise this and create this cadre, as you mentioned—cadre of cyber-trained officers who can be the pointy end of the spear so they can go and actually do the diplomatic efforts in the field and work with my office.

Senator GARDNER. We have developed, 4 years ago, the International Strategy for Cyberspace. It is now 4 years old. And I guess some people are starting to talk about doing some kind of a review, update. Do you believe that that is necessary? And is that something that you can commit to the committee that we would be able to pursue?

Mr. PAINTER. So, I actually—if you look at the international strategy—and I was deeply involved in it, as you know—that was really a high-level vision document. It really laid out what the U.S.'s goals were in this area on a very high level. We have been spending the last number of years—not just my office, but across the government—implementing that strategy. Indeed, my written testimony, I think, goes into quite a bit of detail about how we have been doing that over time.

Even looking at that, I would say I do not think that strategy needs to be rewritten or updated. I think we have a strategy. We do not want to spend our time rewriting strategies. We want to make sure we are actually executing on those strategies. And, just looking at the various buckets in that strategy, if you look at everything in that last chapter about our goals, we have been making some significant progress: protecting our networks—for instance, the State Department has been working on making sure the international law is applicable in cyberspace; working on confidence-building measures; working on norms. In law enforcement, we have 14 additional countries that have now joined the Budapest Convention. And that is significant. In Internet governance, we had a very successful meeting in Brazil, the NETmundial meeting, which reaffirmed the idea of multistakeholder governance, and we fended off attempts to really impose U.N. control in that area. In international development, we have done—my office has done quite a bit of capacity-building work in Africa and other regions to try to bring countries up to speed, because the weakest link hurts us as well as them. And then, in Internet freedom, we have launched the Coalition for Freedom Online, which recently had a meeting, which has 26 governments now. We have made significant progress in funding some of those efforts.

So, across the board, if you look at those categories, there has been a lot of work by us, but also a lot of work by interagency partners. I would certainly be happy to spend more time and come back and talk to you about what specific areas of progress we made, but I do not think we need to write a new strategy at this point.

Senator GARDNER. Thank you.

Senator Cardin.

Senator CARDIN. Well, I am not going to get theoretical. And I know this is very, very tough. I am not trying to simplify these problems. They are hard to define, and it is hard to find consistent applications.

But, there is no question that our allies, and the United States, have been attacked by other countries through cyber, and that their efforts have been to compromise our economy and our infrastructure. So, my first question is—and, of course, the United States has the greatest capacity to deal with cyber attacks, of any country in the world. I believe the work that we do is second to none, and our technology is second to none. So, would it be appropriate if a NATO ally, who has been attacked, would call upon article 4 for consultation, or article 5 for help—would that be appropriate, since we are talking about a cyber attack against a NATO ally?

Mr. PAINTER. Well, I should say a couple of things about that.

First, I think it is significant that NATO, not too long ago, during the Lisbon summit, determined that cyber was part of its core mission. And that is really important. I think that it shows an understanding of the threat. They also determined—and this makes a lot of sense—that NATO needs to spend time making sure its own networks are secure. And they have spent a lot of time doing that recently. But, significantly, in the last summit that just occurred in Wales, there were two things in the communique that I think go to your point. One talked about the applicability of international law in cyberspace. And so, it was not just this group that was in the group of government experts in the U.N., but also all the NATO members affirming that. And they also said that article 5 could apply in a cyber environment, but it would apply on a case-by-case basis. You know, how it would apply, when it would apply, we would look at it case by case.

And certainly article 4, when you are doing consultations, you know, that, I think, will and has happened. We had the Estonia attacks, back in 2007, for instance, which is, I think, in many ways, a wake-up call for people, because people had not thought about that before. And Estonia is one of the connected—most connected countries in the world, and one of our close partners, as well.

So, I think NATO clearly has a role, and it is a developing role, in how we respond to this, but we also want to make sure that that is integrated with a lot of our civilian efforts, especially with our European and other allies who are building better cybersecurity strategies and capabilities.

Senator CARDIN. So, how far are we away, timewise, from having a policy in NATO that we will feel comfortable with in regards to how cyber fits into the traditional defense posture of NATO?

I ask that because technology is changing every day, so, by the time we get an agreement, we will be up to the next level of technology, and we will have to start all over again.

Mr. PAINTER. Well, and one of the things I have found in my career is that, yes, technology moves very, very quickly. But, there are also some core concepts. For instance, when I was at the Justice Department and we were updating cyber crime laws, you try to write those laws so they are technology-neutral. You have seen new developments of technology, but the core concepts of how you apply it would be the same.

For NATO, the same, I think, applies. Cyber is a new area for NATO. Cyber had—they spent a lot of time making sure they had the right policies to secure their systems. They have. People in NATO, who are very dedicated to this and very good, who I have met with on a number of occasions, and—you know, and they have done a lot of thinking about, for instance, how these things will apply.

The fact that article 5 would apply on a case-by-case basis is not really surprising, because article 5 has only really been invoked once, as you know. And so, how you apply it and when you apply it, you know, that has to be a factual basis.

I would also say that that goes really beyond NATO. And one of the things that we see is—even in an existing defense agreements, for instance—cyber is a new attack. It does not specify, in those defense agreements, whether or not——

Senator CARDIN. So, I want——

Mr. PAINTER [continuing]. It is some sort of——

Senator CARDIN [continuing]. I want to stop you for a moment, because, in your testimony, you come up with a good recommendation that there be voluntary norms of responsible——

Mr. PAINTER. Right.

Senator CARDIN [continuing]. State behavior during peacetime that would be universally——

Mr. PAINTER. Yes.

Senator CARDIN [continuing]. Appropriate, and that we will keep us all safer if the states adopt it. And then you go on to say that the states should not conduct or knowingly support, online activity that intentionally damages critical infrastructure, et cetera.

All right. Now, let us try and see whether that works.

Mr. PAINTER. Right.

Senator CARDIN. Because there have been efforts to prevent countries from violating international agreements. There have been reports that there has been Internet use to do that. The United States may say, ''Well, that does not fit under that definition.'' Then we talk to a country like Russia or China, and say, ''Wait, why does it not fit into that definition?'' How do you get an agreement as to when it is appropriate and when it is not appropriate to use the Internet to defend your country?

Mr. PAINTER. So, this is obviously a long-term effort. We are still in the beginning of a lot of these discussions. But, with respect to the peacetime norms that you mentioned, norms like——

Senator CARDIN. We are at peace with Russia, we are at peace with China.

Mr. PAINTER. Right. So, these are norms that the United States is promoting. And, quite frankly, they are norms that have already received some endorsement in the international community. These are things that we have proposed in this GGE session in New York. The Australians recently were at the Australian Foreign Minister talked about some of these norms for—using her own language. We have had the Estonians and others beginning to adopt them.

The way norms get adopted over time is, it takes time to build a consensus of more and more like-minded——

Senator CARDIN. So, you are not——

Mr. PAINTER [continuing]. Countries——

Senator CARDIN. Can you answer my question about whether the United States is prepared to enter into a definitive standard that could jeopardize our security needs in using the Internet to defend America?

Mr. PAINTER. No, not at all. I mean, I think these norms were very carefully and importantly drafted——

Senator CARDIN. And how do you justify a Russian interpretation or a Chinese interpretation that, under national security, they are doing things that clearly violate our understanding of international law?

Mr. PAINTER. Well, and that is exactly it. I mean, that is why we are trying to build this consensus about what these international norms are. Below the threshold of armed conflict, which is a very high threshold where international law applies, and we are trying to determine exactly how it applies in this space. These are norms that are, I think, more applicable, because this is the kind of thing we see every day. They are not universally accepted yet. These are new norms that we are putting out there and we are trying to get a consensus of countries around. This is very similar to other areas. And one of the examples I have used in the past is the Proliferation Security Initiative, as a model.

Senator CARDIN. I was going to give that example——

Mr. PAINTER. Well——

Senator CARDIN. Is it all right for us—I mean, will——

Mr. PAINTER. Well, so——

Senator CARDIN. There will be disagreements as to whether we can use the Internet and cyber to enforce proliferation commitments.

Mr. PAINTER. Well, this is exactly—you know, this is the kind of process you undertake so that you build a greater consensus around these norms, which—you know, these norms are not written just to protect the United States. These norms are written because they are universally applicable. They are attractive to all countries, including countries we may disagree with on a lot of substantive areas. Not attacking critical infrastructures that provide services to the public when you are at peacetime is one that is pretty—it should be pretty acceptable to many countries.

The second part of the question, I think, is then: How do you enforce them, assuming you get that agreement? And I think that is where I use as an example the Proliferation Security Initiative, where you have a group of like-minded countries, and if people are outside that group, you can use a number of ways to try to enforce those actions. And that is pretty far down the road, I admit. I would say our efforts—there is a number of parts of our effort. Part of it is the technical and the other ways that we are trying to meet these threats now. Part of it is to shape the international environment, which is what the norms are. And part of it is confidence-building measures, which are more short term, to build more transparency and understanding, and even things like hotlines so we can try to head some of these off.

But, none of these, on their own, is a complete solution. They have to be put together.

Senator CARDIN. Thank you.

Senator GARDNER. I think, if you do not mind, we will just go back, another round, if you do not mind, just——

Mr. PAINTER. Sure, go ahead.

Senator GARDNER [continuing]. Just to follow up on the question of these norms that we are talking about, because I think it is difficult to say that we have certain redlines. I do not think you can say—are there any redlines that we have in cyber? That is what the norms are trying to get to. But, is there any—can we, right now, say that there is a redline in cyber that somebody could cross and we would have a response?

Mr. PAINTER. Well, I mean, I think, just like in the physical realm, there are things that are—you do not create strict redlines for deterrence, for instance, because you do not want to say people—you do not want people creeping up to that redline and then not acting.

I think, just like in the physical world, there is interpretation that you would do. On some of these issues, though, these are things that we would say should be condemned. So, if you are at peacetime, and you attack the critical infrastructure of another country that is being used to provide services to the public, we would say that that is something that should not be allowed, that the international community could work against—should sanction that and work against that. We would say that the theft of intellectual property to benefit your commercial sector is something that we do not do, it should not be allowed. We would say that, you know, if you attack the CCERT of another country, the Computer Emergency Response Team, that is inherently destabilizing. That should not be allowed. So, we are trying to create that framework.

When you get to the higher level of international law that applies to conflict, of course there are different rules there. There is the U.N. Charter, there is the Law of Armed Conflict. There has been a lot of work, and it is continuing. And how that actually applies, our Department, in concert with our DOD and other Departments throughout the government, have been putting some thoughts forward on how it would apply, but that is still an ongoing process.

Senator GARDNER. And how much of these conversations are drawn to something around what is a use of force when it comes to a cyber threat or attack?

Mr. PAINTER. That certainly is one of the things that is being discussed. But, you know, even in the physical world, you do not necessarily define exactly what a use of force is. I mean, sometimes it will depend on the factual elements. And some of the things that we put forth in our submission, which I am happy to share with you, talk about some of the factors you may look at.

Senator GARDNER. And then North Korea, I think, was taken off of the State Sponsor of Terror List in around 2008. What in the cyber world would elevate to the point that it is reconsidered for being put back on that list? Cyber vandalism, I think, was described—the President described the Sony attack. What would rise to the level of a relisting of a nation like North Korea?

Mr. PAINTER. Well, I think it is important to note that the administration took some pretty strong action in the North Korea case. First of all, really, in an unprecedented way, the President came out and condemned the attack and named North Korea as the actor. And a number of other countries also condemned that attack. And that was very significant.

Secondly, the President issued a sanctions order—a North Korea-specific sanctions order—that dealt with North Korea more broadly, not just for the cyber activity, but also for a range of destabilizing activity they have been involved in.

With respect to listing a terrorism, that is a very—you know, that is a specified issue, and there are certain criteria that are used as that is being considered. As I understand it, as a matter of law, to be designated, the Secretary of State has to determine that the government of that country has repeatedly provided support for acts of international terrorism, and they are made after very careful review, and there is a process for that. And, of course, we regularly review available intelligence on North Korea to determine whether the facts indicate that it should be designated as a state sponsor of terrorism.

So, that said, I think we have to look at the larger context, not just in the cyber world, but more generally.

Senator GARDNER. But, I mean, obviously, cyber is going to be more and more a part of those kinds of conversations.

Mr. PAINTER. I think it will be. I shy away from using the term, frankly, ''cyber terrorism,'' because I do not know what that term means, often. There is terrorist use of the Internet to plan——

Senator GARDNER. Should we develop a meaning for it, though? Should we know what it is?

Mr. PAINTER. No. I mean, I think we just use specificity when we are talking about these issues. I use ''cyber attacks'' or ''cyber intrusions.'' That is one. And they could be terrorist sponsored. We have not really seen a lot of cyber attacks by terrorists. We really have not seen that. We certainly have seen terrorists use the Internet to plan, to promote, to raise money, all of those things. That is more terrorist use of the Internet. I think we just need to be careful in how we are using the terms, because people—you know, there are other states—Russia and China sometimes will use cyber terrorism to mean far different things than we mean, meaning, you know, groups that disagree with the government. And that is not what a cyber terrorist is.

Senator GARDNER. On April 1, 2015, the President did issue his Executive order establishing punitive tools to deal with cyber crime. It is good for a start. We have significant threats, though, from other actors out there, a precedent for—and we have well-known threats—setting precedent for imposing previous financial penalties against bad actors, like designations of the PLA hackers, lots of opportunities for us to impose such actions. Why did the President's Executive order not couple actual designation of entities? And has the State Department and the Treasury Department—do you have a belief that there are people who meet the criteria for imposing such penalties?

Mr. PAINTER. So, the point of the Executive order—and again, having been at this for a long time in different capacities—was to make sure we had a new tool, to make sure we had a new arrow in our quiver to deal with these various threats out there. Certainly, we have criminal law that is out there now. We have other capabilities. We have diplomatic tools. But, we recognized, especially when those tools were inadequate and we had a very significant threat, we needed to have and develop this new tool. And it is important that actual deals within a range of different actions, significant actions—and the threshold is pretty high—cyber activity, including destructive attacks, including intrusions, including theft of intellectual property, and the receipt of stolen intellectual property.

So, it was important to get that framework in place before we start thinking about what the designations are. Now, I would say that that order is not limited—I mean, it is targeted, so it is individuals or entities, but it is not limited to, you know, criminal groups or nation-states. It could be any group or individual within that category. And we are looking very carefully at what designations we will make under that order now that we have that tool in place. That is something that the State Department is involved in, Treasury is involved in, Justice is involved in; and, frankly, other agencies are, too.

Senator GARDNER. Okay. And can you share with the committee right now any considerations that you are making for either entities or individual designations?

Mr. PAINTER. I really cannot right now. This is an ongoing process. It is something we take very seriously. We obviously developed this tool because it is a tool we thought was necessary, and we are looking at how to apply it.

But, I would say, again, that it is one of the tools we have. We have other tools, too. And we have used some of those other tools, like the law enforcement tool that you mentioned. And we certainly used the diplomatic tool, for instance, when we called out North Korea and we have called out China for theft of intellectual property.

Senator GARDNER. Senator Cardin.

Senator CARDIN. Let me make a suggestion to you. On page 11 of your written report and during your presentation, near the end, you mentioned the work that we are doing in regards to promoting Internet freedom and human rights online. And I appreciate that.

You also mentioned the fact that you and Tom Malinowski just returned from a Freedom Online Coalition meeting in Mongolia. And I very much appreciate that issue.

But, on page 8, where you list international norms that we are striving for, you do not mention the human rights, freedom-of-information dimension. If the United States does not mention it, it will not get mentioned. We are the leader on this. And, recognizing what is happening in China today on this "Great Cannon," which really has me greatly concerned, where they are trying to conduct censorship through the use of cyber, it seems to me that the United States must be the leader on promoting Internet freedom and access to information. And I just would hope you would make that a more visible part of your presentation.

Mr. PAINTER. Let me just say that that is a core part of our policy. Not only is it a core part of our policy, it is reflected in the international strategy. It is a very important part of the international strategy. As we look at all of these different security issues, we make sure we are looking at that, too. We should never use security as a proxy for controlling speech. And we are being very careful about that. And that is one of the reasons that my office and the office that Tom Malinowski heads really work hand in glove on these issues.

I should say, the norms you mentioned back in that particular paragraph, those were norms that were political military norms for cyber stability. We are champions of Internet freedom, particularly on very important norms that dealt with—there was a Human Rights Commission—or committee resolution a couple of years ago that said that, at core, you have the same rights online as you do offline. That is something that we have advanced, that is something we have worked with our colleagues around the world for. Internet freedom really is—and I assure you—a core part of our policy that is reflected in, really, everything we do. So, this is not something that is a sideline for us.

Senator CARDIN. I am going to take issue with you. You mentioned, on page 9, the work of the OSCE. And I appreciate that. The OSCE's principles are that human rights and economic security is all part of the security of a country, and very much part of a defense posture. I would argue that Internet freedom and human rights issues are very much a matter for the military to be concerned about, because it does lead to violence, and it does lead to the use of our military. So, I would hope that it would be showcased in all of our portfolios on cybersecurity.

Mr. PAINTER. And, Senator, I assure you it is. In the OSCE, as you know, there is a portion that deals with some of the political military issues. The Law of Armed Conflict and international humanitarian law deals with a lot of these issues when you get to conflict. And that is why it is important to say there are rules in cyberspace. It is not a lawless area. And this is something that really, in a very strong way, we have promoted everywhere.

One of the things we have done is, we have worked with our colleagues at DRL to make sure that more countries are joining this Freedom Online Coalition. When I go out and talk to other countries, when I have my bilaterals with other countries, I conduct these all-of-government bilaterals. One of the people at the table with me is from our human rights shop. One of the things that we advance is, ''Please join this coalition, look at these different issues together. Do not think about security in a silo, so you are just doing security. Think about the issues that relate to freedom online and the free flow of information.'' That is really core to what we do.

Senator CARDIN. All I am suggesting is, make it more visible, because, if you do not do it, no other country will. This is——

Mr. PAINTER. We are——

Senator CARDIN [continuing]. The United States——

Mr. PAINTER. We are the champions and the leaders on this, and we will continue to be, yes.

Senator CARDIN. I appreciate that.

Now, let me ask you about your working with the private sector. My own experiences in trying to figure out how we can deal with legislation here—you know, on the Hill—it is very difficult, with the private sector. They are not that anxious to harmonize with government on how their information is protected. They are not interested in reporting to us violations that have occurred to them, because they are either somewhat embarrassed or worried that it could be used against them from a commercial point of view. So, do you have any suggestions on how we are going to be able to develop the type of working relationship with the private sector, which is critically important, to advance our common goals?

Mr. PAINTER. Yes. So, I have had a long history with the private sector. First of all, the private sector, as you know, is not monolithic, it is not ''the private sector.'' It is lots of different entities, just like government's not monolithic. And one of the core things that we did when I was at the White House, when I was at Justice, and certainly at State, is that we worked very closely with the private sector. We recognized that we do not see every opportunity or, frankly, every risk that is out there when we do these diplomatic outreach efforts, when we try to build these groups. So, in a number of different ways, we have consulted with the private sector, even with respect to the international strategy. This is something I briefed to them before we finalized it. And we include them in a lot of our different policies.

We also included them, as I mentioned, when we did the training for all the officers around the world. We had private-sector people there and panels who talked to them about this part of the equation. And when we have done a lot of the training for other countries, especially in Africa, we have had a private-sector component. So, the private sector has been—and civil society, as well—have been a key component to this.

I do think that there has been a lot of efforts—and I know there is a lot of legislation on the Hill now, including legislation that the administration has been pushing, in terms of more sharing of vulnerability information between the private sector and the government—I think that is heading in the right direction. I think we want to make sure that we can get that and we can share it. Private-sector information-sharing has been an issue for as long as I have been doing this, and I think I have seen a real uptick on that. I have seen some good collaborative efforts. For instance, the Department of Homeland Security has their floor, their response floor, and the private sector participates in that. When we did the National Cyber Incident Response Plan, the private sector helped build that from the beginning.

So, I think there are real important partners in all of this. And, yes, there are different voices in the private sector, but I think we are moving in the right direction now to get the kind of information-sharing we need.

I do think that is critical. I think, without information-sharing, it is going to be very difficult for government to do its job, not just in the United States, but around the world.

Senator CARDIN. Thank you.

Thank you, Mr. Chairman.

Senator GARDNER. Thank you, Mr. Painter. And I have got just a couple of more questions for you. I do not want to keep you here all day, because I know we have another panel and we have got votes coming up at noon, so I do not want to keep you here too long.

Just a couple of questions on China. You know, I think, in a report in 2013, Admiral Blair, Ambassador Huntsman cited a number—I think it was pretty stunning—$300 billion a year, they believe, in terms of theft through cyber—cyber theft around the globe annually to the United States—$300 billion. And I think, under their estimates, 50 to 80 percent is—broad range, but still a very high number—actually, they believe could be directed or attributed to China as a result of that $300 billion. And so, how do you, as the State Department, then, following up on this conversation with the private sector—how do you work with China to address these theft concerns?

Mr. PAINTER. So, again, it is an all-of-government solution. We look at a lot of different—or problem—and we look at a lot of different tools. I think, you know, the United States has had serious concerns about Chinese state-sponsored cyber-enabled theft of trade secrets and commercial gain for some time. As part of our response to this threat, we have worked with industry to encourage the strengthening of their own defenses, so, essentially, hardening the targets and make sure they have the information and share the information they need to prevent these attacks and intrusions.

We have also directly confronted the Chinese about this activity and the threats they pose to the bilateral relationship with the United States and U.S. economic competitiveness and, frankly, China's global reputation and their own economic competitiveness in the long term. This was done at the highest level. As you know, the President has called this out, and the National Security Advisor—many senior Department officials. And we have raised this with them in things like the strategic security dialogue, in the S&ED, as part of our overall relationship, as something that is an important thing to consider.

And we are also working with a number of like-minded governments, because we are not the only victims of these kinds of intrusions, and we want to make sure the governments understand the scope of this problem and are taking it seriously, as well.

I would note that the recent meeting of Prime Minister Abe with the President when he was here—if you look at the statement, there is a pretty hefty part of that statement that deals with cyber, including norms and how we are going to work together on norms, but also how we are going to share information to better protect against the theft of intellectual property. So, that is another thing we are doing.

You mentioned the indictment—the five—you know, the indictment of the five PLA officers. That is another tool we can use. And, of course, we are going to look at all the tools we have. But, this is something that we are going to continue to press. We need to continue to press this issue, because it is important to the United States and important to other economies around the world. At the same time, we have to also try to find ways to work with the Chinese productively, because they are the other—you know, they are one of the biggest actors in cyberspace. And when we are talking about issues like fearing miscalculation or a misperception in escalation in cyberspace, it is important for them and us to be—you know, for them to be responsible members of the world community. And that is why we are putting forth these norms and trying to advance these confidence-building measures. We had a cyber working group, which, you know, I think was unfortunate that it was suspended by the Chinese after the indictments. I led that group. It is important to have these conversations so we can express these concerns clearly, but, at the same time, deal with issues where we need to build collaboration, including exchange of technical information from CERTs, in cybersecurity.

You know, I think when—I want to pivot it for a second to the—one of the norms we have talked about, which is the norm against cyber-enabled intellectual property theft. That is going—that is part of the longer term effort, getting more and more countries to say that that is something that we support, that is something that really, if you are acting outside of that, you are outside of the world norm on that. So, that is part of these efforts, too.

But, this is going to be something we are going to continue to press, quite frankly.

Senator GARDNER. And just, quickly, what are your thoughts on the Russia-China cyber pact last week?

Mr. PAINTER. Well, you know, I think there are a couple of interesting things about that. We are looking at that, certainly, but I would say that it evidences some things that are not too surprising in terms of the way Russia and China look at cyberspace. They have a very absolutist view of sovereignty in cyberspace, that, essentially, you can draw a sovereign boundary around cyberspace, and it applies to everything that goes on within that boundary. And I think it is indicated in that agreement. And we hold a different view. We believe that sovereignty does apply in cyberspace, to an extent, but it does not transcend things—to go to Senator Cardin's question—like the Universal Declaration of Human Rights. That is a norm. The Universal Declaration of Human Rights guarantees human rights and speech across borders, and it does not matter—you cannot draw a sovereign boundary around that. So, it indicates a very different view of them versus us.

It also—they use the term ''information security'' vice ''cybersecurity.'' We talked about protecting networks. They are worried about the destabilizing nature of information.

So, I would say, you know, that is the way we analyze it. More broadly, this indicates why we need to be very active, diplomatically, around the world, because certainly there are many countries that adopt the vision that we put in the international strategy, the vision of an open Internet with security, interoperability, all together. You do not have to trade one off for the other. But, there are many other countries, particularly in the developing world, that are struggling, they are on the fence, they see the benefits of stability, and they are worried about that. And we need to work with those countries—and this is why capacity-building is so important—to make sure that they understand that the vision that we are putting forth is good for them. It is good for them economically, it is good for them socially. And so, as we go forward in all these different international organizations—cyber is being debated everywhere around the world now, in every organization you can think about—we need to make sure that we are reaching out to the countries who are not the traditional allies, who are the countries who are now just getting Internet access and who are dealing with some of these issues.

Senator GARDNER. Thank you, Mr. Painter. Thank you for your service and your testimony today.

And, Senator Cardin, I do not think you have anything else?

Senator CARDIN. Thank you.

Senator GARDNER. Thank you.

And if I could ask the—we are finished with the first panel now, and if I could ask the witnesses to the second panel, please come forward.

On our second panel, we have two distinguished witnesses from the private sector to give us outside perspective on U.S. Government efforts and our policies.

Our first witness is Mr. Jim Lewis, who serves as the senior fellow and program director of the Strategic Technologies Program at the Center for Strategic and International Studies. Before joining CSIS, he worked at the Department of State and Commerce as a Foreign Service officer and as a member of the Senior Executive Service. His government experience includes work on Asian political-ical military issues as a negotiator on conventional arms and technology transfers, and on military and intelligence-related technologies.

Welcome, Mr. Lewis. Thank you for being here.

And our second witness today is Prof. Michael Greenberger, who is founder and director of the University of Maryland's Center for Health and Homeland Security and a professor at the University of Maryland Francis King Carey School of Law, where I think Senator Cardin admitted he may still have a student loan. [Laughter.]

He is currently——

Senator CARDIN. It was a lot cheaper—I am embarrassed at what the fees were when I went to law school compared to today. I think my law-school books were more expensive than tuition. That has changed.

Senator GARDNER. He is currently a member of the Baltimore-Washington Cyber Task Force, serves on the Commission on Maryland Cybersecurity Innovation and Excellence, is a member of the American Bar Association's Law and National Security Advisory

Committee and a member of the National Academy's Committee on Science, Technology, and Law. Previously, Professor Greenberger also served in the Department of Justice and the Commodity Futures Trading Commission.

Welcome, Professor Greenberger.

And I would ask, Mr. Lewis, if you would begin, 5 minutes, then we will turn to you, Professor Greenberger. But, thank you very much for your testimony today. And your full statement, of course, will be entered into the record.

With that, Mr. Lewis, recognize you for testimony.

STATEMENT OF JAMES ANDREW LEWIS, DIRECTOR AND SENIOR FELLOW, STRATEGIC TECHNOLOGIES PROGRAM, CENTER FOR STRATEGIC AND INTERNATIONAL STUDIES, WASHINGTON, DC

Mr. LEWIS. Thank you, Chairman Gardner and Senator Cardin. I would like to thank the committee for this opportunity to testify.

Cybersecurity is a new challenge for foreign policy. It has reshaped economies—the Internet and other cyber technologies have reshaped economies and accelerated growth, providing immense benefit. But, they can also be used for malicious purposes. Digital networks provide countries with new ways to grow and to trade with each other, but they are also a means of influence, coercion, and attack.

Four countries—Russia, Iran, North Korea, and China—are our principal rivals in cyberspace. To constrain them, we need better defenses, we need penalties for malicious action, and we need international agreement on the rules for responsible state behavior. Getting these rules requires the support of our allies and new regional powers, like India and Brazil.

The U.S. approach to international cybersecurity is to seek agreement on norms and to create confidence-building measures and build mechanisms for cooperation. Norms and CBMs are really the best approach available. A cyber treaty would be unenforceable. We cannot deter our adversaries. Deterrence does not work against espionage or crime. And it may not work at all against state actors like ISIS or other terrorist groups.

The United States is, as you heard, involved in many discussions on cybersecurity in the U.N. and in regional groups, such as the OSCE, but progress has been slow. The United States has had more success in revising its mutual security treaties with our allies in Asia and with NATO to make cybersecurity a part of collective defense.

Cyberspace is a man-made environment operated by commercial companies. This complicates the efforts to reach agreement on security. And, while there is international agreement that the private sector should play a role in cybersecurity and that this role should reflect private-sector competencies in technology and business, many countries would still prefer that nation-states lead in any negotiation.

This administration issued an international cyber strategy in 2011. I believe it is time to rethink this strategy, in light of a very different international situation. This is a much more difficult negotiating environment than we faced 4 years ago, and we have much more vigorous rivals who have, as you pointed out with the recent agreement between Russia and China, come up with an alternate approach that challenges the United States.

The principal issue for reconsideration in the U.S. strategy is whether to seek agreement first among like-minded countries or to continue to wait for some broad global agreement. The United States has been reluctant to adopt a like-minded approach, although that is what we used in proliferation and arms control, fearing that we will lose the support of important countries like India or Brazil. But, the difference now is that we face a determined effort by Russia and China to dismantle American leadership in international affairs, not just cybersecurity, but across the board, and it will be difficult to reach agreement with these rivals on any cybersecurity issue.

The Department of State also needs to rethink how it is organized for cybersecurity. They were the leaders in creating a coordinator. The rest of the world has copied them. Now it is time to think if we need a more formal and permanent organization within the Department.

In the last decade, cybersecurity has become a central issue for international security and diplomacy. Given its importance for our economy, for trade, for national security, I think the committee is doing exactly the right thing by picking this up. And cybersecurity should be part of the foreign policy agenda for this Congress.

Now I am going to do one thing that I had not written in my remarks, but I am going to give you a simple measure for success. That measure is that Russia and China, between the two of them, are probably responsible for more than two-thirds of the malicious cyber actions we see undertaken against the United States. They are, by and far, our largest rivals, they are the most active, they do the most damage. And a good measure for success is: Is the Russian and Chinese share of malicious cyberactions decreasing? If the answer is no, what we are doing is not working. With that, Mr. Chairman, that happy, positive finish——

[Laughter.]

Mr. LEWIS [continuing]. Thank you for the opportunity to testify, and I will be happy to take any questions.

[The prepared statement of Mr. Lewis follows:]

PREPARED STATEMENT OF JAMES ANDREW LEWIS

I would like to thank the committee of this opportunity to testify.

Cybersecurity is a new challenge for foreign policy. The Internet and other cyber technologies have reshaped economies and accelerated growth, providing immense benefit, but like any tool it can be used for purposes good or bad. Digital connections provide countries with new ways to grow and trade, but they are also a means of coercion, influence, and attack. Exploiting computer networks has become another tool for state power and competition. Countries use the Internet and cyberspace to gain advantage over others. The use of cyber tools and techniques as an instrument of national power is now the norm. Getting international agreement on how states should behave in cyberspace is essential, but it will also be difficult.

The first known examples of what we would now call cyber espionage occurred in the early 1980s, when the KGB hired German hackers to break into U.S. military research computer networks. The first use of cyber attack for military purposes occurred in the mid 1990s, when the U.S. used primitive cyber attack tools against Serbia. In the late 1990s, Chinese military writings discussed cyber attack as a means to gain asymmetric advantage over the United States. Perhaps this flurry of military activity led Russia in 1998 to introduce in the U.N. a treaty to limit the development and use of cyber weapons.

The draft treaty drew extensively on Russia's experience with strategic arms control. One precedent may have been the 1960's Outer Space Treaty, which establish principles of state responsibility and banned nuclear and other weapons of mass destruction from space. The analogy between space and outer space is inexact however, despite rhetoric about there being no borders in cyberspace. It is difficult to gain access to space and the technology, particularity in the 1960s, was expensive and limited to only a handful of nations. In contrast, the technologies needed for malicious action in cyberspace are ubiquitous and easily acquired. Clandestine operations are particularly easy in cyberspace. Nor do cyber attacks pose the risk of horrific effect similar to nuclear weapons, which created a shared desire for restraint even among opponents.

The very covertness of cyber action works against international agreements on security, and until 2010, there was no progress on international agreement. There was too much distrust among competing nations for a treaty. The technology was also very new, and there was a general unfamiliarity in the international community with cybersecurity as a national security issue. The U.S. only began to consider diplomatic solutions in the last few years.

Some of this slow start reflects a too-great reliance on the technical community to manage cybersecurity. The problems we face are not technical; they are political and requires policy and diplomatic skills to make progress. Some of the slow start reflects the millennial beliefs of the 1990s about the Internet and the future of international relations. It seems hard to believe, but in the 1990s people believed that with the end of the cold war, the world would become one big market democracy with shared values and no borders. Governments would play a smaller role in global affairs and could be replaced by a collection of civil society organizations and multinational corporations in some multistakeholder process. Those who believed this dream had a rude awakening in 2001 and while things have not gotten better since then, many in the Internet community cling to these shattered beliefs.

OPPONENTS

For the U.S., better cybersecurity requires changing the behavior of four countries. Russia is the principle source of cyber crime and extremely active in political-military espionage, and is the most skilled opponent we face. China leads in economic cyber espionage. Iran has developed significant cyber capabilities and uses them to apply political pressure on the U.S. It has also done the network reconnaissance necessary to launch cyber attacks against critical infrastructures, as have China and Russia. North Korea has invested for decades in building cyber attack capabilities. There are also jihadist groups who have rudimentary cyber capabilities. Hezbollah and the Syrian Electronic Army are connected to Iran and through Iran, perhaps to Russia. ISIS, with its sophisticated Internet skill, bears watching carefully as a group that could develop the capability for low-level attack.

Dealing with these countries also requires a broad diplomatic strategy to win support from key allies and from emerging new powers, like Brazil, India, and others. These new powers from a middle ground between western democracies and authoritarian regimes, and the policies these countries choose to pursue will determine the future of the Internet and cybersecurity. Most of the new powers support fundamental human rights, and in particular freedom of speech and free access to information. This puts them at odds with the authoritarian view of cyberspace, but they also believe that national sovereignty and government must play a larger role in Internet matters, and they were troubled by the NSA revelations, factors that work against U.S. influence. To win the global support, the U.S. needs persuasive arguments on privacy, Internet governance, and the use of force in cyberspace. We do not now have these persuasive arguments and some of what we say now about the Internet is seen as duplicitous. The NSA leaks of the last 2 years, whose selective release is used intentionally to damage the U.S., have not helped us.

Cybersecurity is a military and intelligence contest with dangerous opponents. There are significant trade issues. The Internet has immense political effect that threatens authoritarian regimes and has led them to mount significant challenges to market and democratic ideals and the international institutions created to support them. The focal point of this challenge is to reduce U.S. influence, not just over the Internet but also in trade, security, and finance. We face a determined effort to dismantle American leadership in international affairs.

DETERRENCE

There is a hope that the U.S. could use military force to deter malicious cyber activity, but this has not been effective. Deterrence was the linchpin of U.S. strategy for decades, but the political and military context for deterrence has changed significantly. Instead of a single, near-peer opponent, the U.S. faces an array of possible foes, each with differing capabilities and tolerances for risk. Deterrence is of much less utility as a guide for policy in this new environment.

Deterrence requires opponents to compare the benefits of an action against the potential cost and assess the likelihood that such costs will actually be imposed. There must be credible threats that if a threshold or "redline" is crossed, it will lead to unacceptable loss. In the cold war, the threat of nuclear war deterred the Soviets from invading Western Europe and Japan or launching strategic attacks against the U.S. While it was often a subject of debate, the nuclear "umbrella" set redlines the Soviets could understand and found credible because they were linked to core American interests. The U.S. has thresholds or declaratory policies, but they are surrounded by a mass of caveats. This is sometimes lauded as "strategic ambiguity," but in fact, our adversaries just find it confusing. If opponents do not know what lines they should not cross, or do not believe that we will penalize them for crossing those lines, it will be hard to deter them.

Our most active opponents also seek to circumvent deterrence. They look for tactics that stay below this ill-defined threshold that allow them to damage the U.S. without triggering retaliation. They believe that the U.S. will also build new weapons, including cyber weapons that will allow it to circumvent their own deterrent forces and strike them with impunity. While we can be confident that our nuclear and conventional forces will deter major attacks on the U.S. and it sallies, it will not deter challenges in Crimea or he South China Sea, terrorism, or malicious cyber activities. Even nuclear threats in the cold war did not stop Soviet espionage or regional adventures and we cannot deter cyber espionage or cyber crime. A different approach is required to bring security and stability to cyberspace. This is important because deterrence, if it works, if unilateral and does not require international agreement. The ineffectiveness of unilateral deterrence increases the need for international agreement.

U.S. DIPLOMATIC STRATEGY

Getting international agreement is what the 2011 International Strategy for Cyberspace tries to do. This administration is the first to have a published international strategy for cyberspace, which it released in 2011. That strategy now needs significant reconsideration since we are now in a very different political environment, less peaceful, more challenging, and with overt opposition.

The U.S. diplomatic strategy for cybersecurity is based on the building cooperation among countries and reaching agreement on norms and confidence-building measures (CBMs). Its starting point is recognition that a cybersecurity treaty is not possible. The core of the strategy is agreement on norms for responsible state behavior in cyberspace. Unlike a treaty, norms are not legally binding. They reflect instead international expectations about state behavior. The normative builds on the experience of nonproliferation. With the Missile Technology Control regime, for example, a few like-minded nations (NATO, Japan, and Australia) agreed that responsible states do not transfer ballistic missile technology. Eventually the number of adherent nations grew and there was acceptance of a new global norm of behavior, including, after several decades, a measure of formal agreement. A similar process helped to create norms for chemical and biological weapons.

There are already implicit norms governing cyber conflict that are derived from existing international law and practice. Making these norms explicit and expanding, their scope would increase stability. The argument that norms are too weak can be dismissed as there is no serious alternative. Legally binding commitments have serious drawbacks. Our most likely adversaries will just ignore treaties. Treaties face serious implementation problems involving compliance and verification. Nonstate actors have limited influence over major states, cannot themselves commit their country to an agreement, and lack legal standing under international law. The existing "state of nature" is too Hobbesian to be sustained as the Internet and other digital networks become the most essential of global infrastructures. A norms based approach offers the greatest chance for progress.

There is now agreement among most countries that existing internal commitments apply in cyberspace as they did in the physical domain. Gaining this agreement has been a multifaceted effort, with work in the Organization for Security Cooperation in Europe (OSCE), the ASEAN Regional Forum (ARF), and the Organization of American States (OAS), the forum for Asia-Pacific Economic Cooperation (APEC), the "London Process," and the U.N. to develop confidence-building measures and norms. Work to win greater acceptance of the Budapest Convention on cyber crime reinforces the central concept of "normalizing" cyberspace by defining state responsibilities toward other states and their citizens. While there are regional differences (certainly in pace, if not substance), there is an emerging consensus about responsible state behavior in cyberspace that is consistent with existing norms and commitments among states.

The 2010 and 2013 Reports of the U.N. Group of Governmental Experts (GGE) has been foundational. Russia first proposed GGEs in the early 2000s. The first GGE failed to reach agreement. The second GGE (2010) produced a short report that called on the international community to further develop norms and CBMs (as well as to build capacity in developing countries). While short, this 2010 report laid out the agenda for international discussion of cybersecurity, identifying the application of international law, the development of norms and CBMS, and measures to promote capacity-building, as the core elements of an international approach to stability and security in cyberspace.

The third GGE-produced agreement among countries as diverse as the major NATO allies, Russia, India, and China (albeit reluctantly) that the principle of sovereignty applied to cyberspace, that the commitments to the U.N. Charter, existing international law (including the laws of armed conflict) and commitments to protect universal human rights all applied in cyberspace. While the implications of sovereignty for cyberspace are complex, the physical infrastructure that supports cyber activities is generally located in sovereign territory and is subject to the State's territorial jurisdiction. The agreement on the applicability of sovereignty and international law has fundamentally changed the political landscape for the discussion of cybersecurity, but it is only an initial step in defining how States will act in cyberspace. A fourth GGE is currently underway.

To increase trust, the U.S. has also promoted agreement on a series of confidence-building measures (CBMs). CBMs are a normal diplomatic measure to reduce tension and suspicion. CBMs strengthen international peace and security. They can increase transparency, cooperation, and stability. Building confidence through greater transparency in doctrine, either bilaterally or in multilateral exchanges, could reduce the chance of miscalculation or inadvertent escalation. The lack of transparency makes it more difficult to reach agreement on norms for responsible state behavior or to limit cyber conflict.

The development and agreement on CBMS have had the most success in the OSCE, where cold war precedents and participant experience with arms control created familiarity with such measures. In other regions of the world, where there is less experience with security negotiations, there has been less progress, but there are significant efforts to develop CBMs underway in the ASEAN Regional Forum and the Organization of American States.

Work by the OSCE has been foundational in defining CBMs. These CBMs focus on transparency and coordination. Voluntarily measures agreed ad ref in the OSCE include the provision of national views on cyber doctrine, strategy, and threats. OSCE members will also share information on national organizations, programs, or strategies relevant to cybersecurity, identify a contact point to facilitate communications and dialogue on ICT-security matters, and establish links between national CERTS. OSCE members discussed how existing OSCE mechanisms, such as the OSCE Communications Network, could be used to facilitate communications on cybersecurity incidents and develop additional measures to reduce the risk of misunderstanding.

The U.S. has worked in the U.N. and regional forums to promote agreement on cybersecurity. It also plays a leading role in the London Process, launched by U.K. Foreign Secretary William Hague, is a series of informal international meetings whose aim is to generate a consensus on responsible behavior in cyberspace. Initially the London process was seen as the vehicle for gathering like-minded nations to agree on norms, but its goals have become more diffuse. There have been four meetings, the last of which (in The Hague), produced a robust Chairman's Report. The next meeting is scheduled for 2017 in Mexico.

The U.S. also worked closely with its allies to make cybersecurity part of its defensive alliances. It has modified it collective defense arrangements with Australia, Korea, and Japan to include cybersecurity. NATO, in its 2014 summit, agreed on when a cyber incident could trigger the collective defence provision of article 5 of the North Atlantic Treaty. The key changes have been to create mechanisms for greater cooperation with allies and to agree that damaging cyber attacks fall under collective defense.

THE ROLE OF THE PRIVATE SECTOR

There is international agreement to involve the private sector in cybersecurity "as appropriate." These last two words—"as appropriate" are the key. The role of the private sector varies by issue. For some issues, such as security negotiations, there is very little the private sector can do. Some countries, particularly China and Russia, do not see private sector actors as equals and believe that companies are tools of U.S. policy, something that says much about how they see their own national companies.

For issues like Internet governance, the private sector is vital. There are three broad sets of actors in Internet governance—states, companies, and civil society organizations. In the past, states played a small role by design. This is changing as states assert their traditional roles. Internet governance is in transition, and what we will end up with, if this is well managed, is something like international finance, where private banks, Finance Ministries, and international institutions make decision about governance. This means that the influence of governments over the Internet will increase and the influence of civil society organizations will shrink.

It can be hard to parse through the rhetoric that surrounds cybersecurity, but one way to think of this is that the Internet is not that different from anything else and people should play the roles they usually play in guiding and securing it. Companies should be responsible for innovation in technology and providing services. Governments cannot do as well. Governments should play their traditional roles, ensuring public safety and law enforcement (including enforcement of contracts, defending citizens, and negotiating with other nations on trade, human rights, and all the other issues. Companies cannot do this, nor should we want them to—their job is to generate return to their shareholder.

The idea of formal cooperation among governments on Internet issues is anathema to the old-school internet community. They fear that rules will harm the "free and open Internet" to which all kinds of miraculous economic powers are ascribed. It is true that the global network has brought us immense economic benefits and offers still more. However, the free and open Internet is long gone. To make cyberspace safe, we need transnational rules, norms, and institutions to manage and reduce risk, using international agreement on a collective approach to reduce risk and increase stability. Some countries will balk at cybersecurity norms, as they balked at norms against nuclear proliferation or money-laundering—but the right blend of incentives and penalties (like indictments in U.S. courts) will help change their minds.

The conflict in this lies between those countries like Russia and China that would like to see governments play a dominant role in cyberspace, in order to control information and minimize the political risk to undemocratic regimes, and those few governments that continue to insists that the informal arrangements for security and governance developed in the 1990s are still adequate. Neither approach is desirable but we have not yet identified an adequate replacement that does not diminish the private sectors role in those areas where their leadership is crucial.

There are several areas for partnership between companies and the government in international cybersecurity. At a company level, cybersecurity is a business decision about how much risk a company is willing to accept and how much they are willing to spend to mitigate this risk. Such decisions are best left to individual companies. In the foreign relations context, this largely involves company decisions about the risk of cyber espionage. Where the government can play an essential role is in helping companies adequately assess risk by providing relevant information and by developing penalties and sanctions for cyber economic espionage.

Similarly, American companies and the government must cooperate in rebuilding trust in American products and services. American information technology companies are often caught in the middle of an awkward debate, as foreign government fear to trust U.S. products while at the same time asking U.S. companies to cooperate with them in providing information. Rebuilding international trust requires a longer discussion that involves new ideas on data protection, encryption, localization, and related issues. These issues fall outside the scope of cybersecurity when it is narrowly defined, but no major decision about cybersecurity can be made without reference to them, but the touchstone should be that our national interest is best served by foreign policies that keep American companies strong, competitive, and secure in cyberspace.

The most difficult question for the role of companies in cybersecurity involves hacking back or active defense. Companies can do what they want on their own networks. Companies can do what their national laws allow on national networks. However, they cannot take action on networks in another country. This is illegal and poses serious political risk, even if a U.S. company uses a third party in countries like Israel.

Remember that Russia and China believe that U.S. companies are a tool of the government. They will interpret hacking back as an attack by the U.S. This poses real risk of retaliation and escalation into armed conflict. Our opponents include the Russian FSB and the Iranian Revolutionary Guard. They are unscrupulous, have a taste for violence, and will not hesitate to use force against an attacker. Cyber attacks can have unpredictable effects. The U.S. has led the way in seeking to have countries observe the rule of law in cyberspace. Hacking back not only undercuts this effort, but could put an American company in an awkward position. What if China, for example, was to ask the FBI to cooperate in an investigation of a hack-back or took out Interpol warrants for U.S. executives? If we say no, it ends any effort to get China to cooperate when we request investigations (as we did with the Sony incident). If we say yes, American executives will go to jail. I understand the frustration with the slow pace of reducing cyber crime, and U.S. efforts could usefully be accelerated, but we do not want amateur mistakes to lead to war or retaliation.

CYBERSECURITY AT THE STATE DEPARTMENT

The U.S. strategy has helped shape the diplomatic strategies of other Western democracies. The global challenge to Western institutions and to U.S.-centric Internet governance from authoritarian states and the effect of the NSA leaks—mean that we must reconsider this strategy and strengthen the organization framework that supports it.

The fundamental point for reconsideration is one that has been discussed for years. Should the U.S. try to win global agreement on cybersecurity norms for responsible state behavior, or should it begin with agreement among like-minded national and then seek to broaden this. Of course, it is possible to pursue both strategies simultaneously, but we now need to recognize that Russia and China are unlikely to agree with us on political issues in any meaningful way. The announcement of a cybersecurity agreement between Russia and China is an example of new and more oppositional policies (as are the recent maneuvers by their tiny flotilla of ships in the Mediterranean). The bilateral cyber agreement itself is largely for show, to annoy the Americans and the West, so we do not want to overstate it, but we also should not expect them to defer to American policy the way they did in the 1990s.

The counter argument against a like-minded approach is that we will lose the "fence sitters," the new powers who are in neither in the Western or the authoritarian camp. This fear results in paralysis. The counterexample used against a like-minded approach is the Budapest Convention on cyber crime, which was negotiated among Western countries and now faces opposition from new powers like India who say that since they were not involved in the negotiation, they cannot accept the agreement. It is also very likely that some of the new powers would refuse to participate if Russia and China are not involved. However, if progress in cybersecurity is held hostage to winning the agreement of authoritarian states, we will not get anywhere anytime soon.

A good way to think about this is to ask what would happen if the U.S. were to agree to condition any action by NATO on winning agreement from Russia or China, or from powerful nonaligned nations. This would be the end of collective security; we would hobble ourselves. While we need to engage with Russia and China, and perhaps some initial arms-control style agreements on cyber warfare are possible, and while we need to engage with, and be respectful of, the view of new powers like India, Brazil, and others, we should not refrain from action until we have their consent.

The NSA leaks had little effect on Russia and China, who either suspected or knew of NSA activities, but they have skillfully exploited them to try and divide the U.S. and key Western allies. Crimea has caused far more damage to international negotiations on cybersecurity. The Russians have suspended the bilateral cybersecurity discussions that drove diplomatic progress, and their evaluation of the usefulness of an agreement limiting cyber attack may have changed as they move into a more militant posture vis-a-vis NATO. Crimea has sharpened interstate conflict, albeit in a hybrid rather than conventional venue, and has greatly reduced the chances for international agreement. Russian strategy has successfully made that country the focal point for agreement on cybersecurity.

A new strategy will need to be complex in that it would require differing kinds of engagements with other countries and a broader range of tools to win progress. It would continue to pursuit of global agreement but seek immediate agreement among like-minded nations on responsible behavior in cyberspace. These understandings should be reinforced by the use of financial sanctions and technological restraints to encourage better behavior and strengthen the rule of law in cyberspace. Precedents from the financial sector are particularly useful, where governments and leading banks work together to develop and follow principles and practices to increase stability and fight crime, suggest a new direction for cyber diplomacy.

A new strategy also requires an institutional underpinning. Cybersecurity is still an appendage within the Department. It is not incorporated into the structure of Bureaus and Under Secretaries State uses for most issues. In an ideal world, cybersecurity would be part of the politico-military Bureau and part of the portfolio of the Under Secretary for International Security Affairs. Arguments could be made that this issue should be placed within the Economics or Global Affairs portfolios, but having sat in many negotiation sessions on cybersecurity, I can affirm that this is a politic-military issue and the negotiators who have done best in negotiations re from an arms control or international law enforcement background.

The U.S. pioneered the creation of cyber coordinators at the White House and at the State Department, an organizational approach many other countries have also copied, and while State has expanded the office of the cyber coordinator, it needs to further embed cybersecurity into the fabric of our diplomacy. Any speech by a senior official on security or trade must mention cybersecurity, and while these officials may not be comfortable with the issue or fluent in its details, they cannot afford to avoid it. The best example of a missed opportunity is the negotiations on Russian entry to the WTO, completed in 2006, when the U.S. secured agreement on tariffs but signally failed to even mention cyber crime. This was a lost opportunity. We know from public examples that the President cares about this issue and has engaged foreign leaders, but there should be some thing between the President and Chris Painter. The Chinese, for example, watch this very closely and if a Cabinet Secretary appears in Beijing and does not mention cybersecurity, they judge it to mean that America is not serious.

You sometimes hear that the issue is too technical or too arcane for senior leaders to discuss. This is not true. Cybersecurity is now a central element of the larger international security agenda, the same way that nonproliferation was a new element 25 years ago, and it is important to embed cybersecurity into American foreign policy the same way that nonproliferation moved from being a technical issue to something of central importance. The Internet is not going to get any less important for economies and security. This is not peripheral issue, particularly as the Internet grows more and more important for our economic life and for international trade and security.

NEXT STEPS

This is a much more difficult negotiating environment, but the biggest obstacle to progress is not recalcitrant authoritarians or skeptical new powers, but what some have called an era of ''strategic timidity'' in the West. If we are afraid of offending Russia, China, or the new powers, we should just accept that while cybersecurity can be improved though better technology and greater attention by companies, it will not be secure against our most effective opponents.

There is always a temptation in American foreign policy to explain the international environment by saying that we are in a ''new cold war'' or to invoke elderly strategies like deterrence or containment to deal with the new challenges we face. We are not in a new cold war. What we face is a more insidious challenge with countries who are our political and military opponents at the same time that they are our economic partners. In an interconnected world, they cannot be contained nor will they be deterred from challenging us. We can no longer blithely assume that we have the moral high ground—China, Russia, and others will challenge our leadership. This is a new kind of contest and we must craft new foreign policies to advance our national interest, the interests of our allies, and of the world. Cybersecurity is among the most salient of these new challenges for American foreign policy and while there has been good progress in the last few years, we need a new a new approach to international agreement on cybersecurity.

In the last decade, cybersecurity has moved from being a peripheral issue or an issue confined to the classified world to one that is central for the internal security and diplomatic agenda. Given its importance for national security, public safety, trade, and development, cybersecurity is the right for the committee to turn its attention to cybersecurity as it thinks about the foreign policy agenda for this Congress.

Thank you for the opportunity to testify and I would be happy to take any questions.

Senator GARDNER. Thank you.
Mr. Greenberger.

STATEMENT OF MICHAEL GREENBERGER, FOUNDER AND DIRECTOR, UNIVERSITY OF MARYLAND CENTER FOR HEALTH AND HOMELAND SECURITY; PROFESSOR, UNIVERSITY OF MARYLAND FRANCIS KING CAREY SCHOOL OF LAW, BALTIMORE, MD

Mr. GREENBERGER. Thank you, Chairman Gardner, Ranking Member Cardin. I am delighted to be here today. The first thing I want to say is, this is a very tough-going area, and it is easy to second-guess and criticize. And I do have suggestions, but by no means do I want to be seen as criticizing the efforts of the State Department or any other Federal agencies. I think sincere good-faith efforts are being made.

But, I would draw an analogy to the train accident in Philadelphia. The train went off the tracks, and there could be a lot of different ways to look at that problem. Was the engineer negligent? Was the engineer criminally negligent? Do we need more laws?

The real thing, I think, needs to be focused on an international basis is, How do we stop the bad things that are happening? I think we can worry later about whether the bad things trigger title 5 of NATO or trigger the laws of war, et cetera, et cetera. What we really have got to do is get a handle on stopping what is going on, and identifying who the perpetrators are.

With regard to international organization, as recently as February 2015, the White House held a summit, and there, there was an echo that is repeated throughout the literature: We need better international cooperation. We have cited the Atlantic Council paper from November 2014 as sort of a model of our concern, but we have adduced certain key principles from that paper that we would suggest be advocated for. And when I say "advocated for," I do not think there needs to be legislation. I do think there needs to be strong congressional oversight to make it clear to the administration what further steps need to be taken to improve international coordination.

The Atlantic Council's number-one priority is collaboration, collaboration on an international basis. My view is that we should not worry about treaties, we should not worry about memos of understanding, but we should go forward and convene the parties who are sympathetic to what we are trying to do to create what I would refer to in the crisis management area, an emergency operations center. Who would the candidates be for cooperation in that? NATO, the European Union, the Atlantic Council, OSCE, OECD, the Organization of American States, and the Organizations of the Pacific Nations. They are all interested in cybersecurity, and I have no doubt the State Department—and I applaud the State Department for everything it is doing—but, we need to bring those groups to the table. It does not need to be an official summit. It just needs to be a convening, on a regular basis, of those groups to exchange information. And, as has been said here, you cannot do this with governmental institutions alone. And there are many active organizations—I would say, for example, the Internet Engineering Task Force, which has laid down norms for preventing cyber attacks—groups of that sort should also be brought to the table. And, in terms of the private parties, the President has identified the critical infrastructure sectors—financial, transportation, health—those parties should be brought to the table, too, on an international basis.

And then, when you sit at the table, what do you do? Number one, Senator Cardin talked about NIST, that we are so pleased to have in Maryland, which has set up a framework for developing defenses to prevent cyber attacks. Is it going to be perfect? No. But, it is better than doing nothing. NIST itself has said that its framework needs to be put into the international sector and discussed among all nations. It has received a lot of high praise for its efforts. And we should make every effort to internationalize it. And that would be the internationalization of norms that are a defense to cyber attacks.

Secondly, the technical organizations that I referred to could be helpful. The biggest problem we have is identifying who is doing the attacking. Now, we can say, generally, Russia and China. But, if you cannot pinpoint where the attack is coming from, it is irrelevant whether we can go after those people with criminal laws or whether we have treaties. The biggest problem in this area is authenticating who is doing the damage. There are other norms that we have suggested.

The final thing I would say is, these are all referred to as confidence-building measures. Traditional confidence-building measures are working with your enemy to build a bonding process so they no longer become your enemy. The hotline with Russia is the foremost example. The confidence-building measures we need now is that the international community—and when I say "international community," let us forget Russia and China and Iran; it is those that are sympathetic to what we are doing—join together to develop norms, methods of identifying perpetrators, identifying infrastructure—the priority of infrastructure that needs to be protected.

We deal, on a daily basis, with responses to crisis management. And I can tell you—look at the Boston Marathon, for example. In the response to that attack, you had the FBI, State police, city police working hand in glove together. That came out of an emphasis by Congress and the various administrations to create these fusions within the State. We have it in Maryland.

The process of just bonding, in and of itself, is therapeutic, because you start discussing things that you can do together. You start learning—city police and FBI never worked well together. In that situation, they worked beautifully together. Why? It is the bonding process of the collaboration.

Thank you.

[The prepared statement of Mr. Greenberger follows:]

PREPARED STATEMENT OF MICHAEL GREENBERGER

INTRODUCTION

My name is Michael Greenberger. I am the Founder and Director of the University of Maryland Center for Health and Homeland Security (CHHS). I have been assisted in the preparation of this statement by Markus Rauschecker, Senior Law and Policy Analyst at CHHS. I am very pleased to have the opportunity to provide this statement to the Senate Foreign Relations Subcommittee on East Asia, the Pacific, and International Cybersecurity Policy on the very important topic of "Cybersecurity: Setting the Rules of the Road for Responsible Global Cyber Behavior."

CHHS is an academic consulting institution that provides guidance in planning, training, and exercises relating to the prevention of, and response to, both man-made and natural catastrophes. CHHS consists of over 50 professionals working on over 90 contracts worldwide. Among CHHS' areas of expertise is the law and policy of cybersecurity. We are involved in academic programs [1] and provide advisory services on legal and policy issues relating to cybersecurity.

THE PROBLEM

Cybersecurity presents a unique policy challenge given the Internet's interconnected global reach and infrastructure. Cybersecurity cannot be ensured through measures based on individual sovereignty or within traditional borders. It is widely recognized that the worldwide scope of the Internet makes dealing with the threat of cyber disruption self-evidently international in nature. Solutions to cyber vulnerability are therefore not only substantive in scope, but require international organization, cooperation, and response.

Unfortunately, the conventional approaches to the solution of other international vulnerabilities do not accommodate themselves to cyberspace. It has been recognized that presently there is not adequate knowledge or agreement on solutions to respond to cyber vulnerabilities, which makes negotiation of effective bilateral or multilateral treaties premature. As our fellow panelist Chris Painter, Coordinator for Cyber Issues at the Department of State, recently stated, the international community is still trying to develop the norms that would be the basis for such treaties.[2]

Disparities in perspectives, as well in the domestic laws of nations in this area, only further complicate the problem. While the temptation exists to find a "silver bullet" response, a global solution of this sort is available neither procedurally or substantively. For example, the oft discussed recommendation of implementing "arms control" in cyberspace is widely recognized as unworkable given the uncertainties in the methods of control.[3] Moreover, it is clear that the problems of cybersecurity not only involve state actors, but private sector actors as well, because much of the world's cyber infrastructure is privately owned and/or operated.

Therefore, the solution cannot be limited to either state actors or private stakeholders alone, but must include a multitude of stakeholders. As the White House has correctly asserted, "the world must collectively recognize the challenges posed by malevolent actors' entry into cyberspace, and update and strengthen our national and international policies accordingly."[4]

While the need for international cooperation to combat cyber threats is widely recognized, it is universally acknowledged that much work needs to be done to promote international solutions. Indeed, enhancing international engagement is a top priority for the Obama administration.[5] Federal officials are calling for greater international cooperation in cyberspace, with the need being especially evident in the area of cyber crime. For example, national law enforcement agencies need to increase information-sharing with international partners to combat international crimes and countries must work together to build up crime fighting capacities.[6]

So, in the face of an overwhelming need and inadequate solutions, the ancient Chinese proverb is apt: a journey of 1,000 miles begins with a single step. We therefore advocate that the U.S. State Department lead a cooperative effort working with sympathetic countries and private stakeholders to begin the development of international crisis management protocols and otherwise establish effective norms to combat international cyber vulnerabilities.

THE SOLUTION

We endorse the suggestion of prominent cyber experts that a step by step approach should be applied to develop highly recommended international confidence-building measures (CBMs) to create an international infrastructure to address cyber vulnerabilities. These CBMs may be created with the support of existing cooperative international entities and private international stakeholder organizations. As a general matter, the United Nations has issued a report endorsing the CBM approach.[7] But, the most detailed outline or plan for the CBM international approach comes from the Atlantic Council's recent November 2014 report on this subject.[8]

We agree with the Atlantic Council report's suggestions of the international stakeholders who are likely allies to this U.S.-directed CBM approach. It may not be possible to engage each of these stakeholder institutions in the first instance, but we think the U.S. State Department should turn to these organizations to see if it can find significant cooperation on all suggested CBM approaches or whether alliances should be formed to address individual-recommended CBMs. Whatever approach is taken, the organizing effort must begin promptly. We agree that even if the organizing structure is not "prefect," i.e., getting cooperation of all stakeholders, whatever organizing structure that can be assembled will generate by its example and effectiveness greater worldwide support.

As suggested above, the international organizational format must be developed by engaging both sympathetic governmental as well as nongovernmental organizations. Examples of international governmental organizations that could promote the CBM approach, would include NATO, the Association of Southeast Asian Nations Regional Forum, the Asia Pacific Economic Cooperation Forum, the Council of Europe, the European Union, the Organization of American States, and the Organization for Security and Cooperation in Europe, each of which has expressed at least a need for international cooperation in this area. Examples of nongovernmental organizations that should be consulted include the Internet Society, Internet Engineering Taskforce, and World Wide Web Consortium.

Additionally, as the Atlantic Council report correctly advises, in cyberspace, important "private-sector actors like the financial system, telecommunications, power grids, and energy infrastructure or critical cybersecurity and information technology companies" must be included in the development of international CBMs.[9] Each of these sectors "has a critical role to play in defending against cyber attacks, so the concept of CBMs must be expanded to include the private sector."[10]

In its November 2014 report, the Atlantic Council has outlined a series of CBMs in four different areas: (1) Collaboration; (2) Crisis Management; (3) Restraint; (4) Engagement. We agree with each of the recommendations made in the report; however, we would give immediate priority to four measures within the aforementioned areas. These four measures are given priority based on the limited obstacles they face in successful implementation and their relative low funding requirements. We believe that important work has been started in each of these areas we focus upon, yet the full accomplishment of these measures would serve as a backbone to international cooperation and responsiveness.

The four measures we see as priorities are as follows:

1. Promulgating and Implementing Cybersecurity Best-Practices Internationally

As the cyber threat has grown, many security measures have already been developed to strengthen cybersecurity across sectors. These measures must be better promoted and more widely implemented. Technical regimes may be leveraged to agree and codify best-practices that should be internationally adopted. It is important to note that the international community would not need to establish entirely new practices, but simply adopt and, where necessary modify, existing practices that are generally accepted. Efforts such as the development of the National Institute of Standards and Technology (NIST) Cybersecurity Framework[11] provide evidence of best-practices that have been well received internationally across the public and private cyber sectors.

Technical regimes may also be called on to identify the international entities that are already implementing existing best-practices. These findings should be publicized in order to praise entities meeting objectives, but also to demonstrate a lack of compliance by others. Essentially, noncomplying entities would be "named-and-shamed" and we believe they would thus be motivated to adopt generally accepted cybersecurity practices.[12]

2. Joint Investigations of Cyber Incidents

The problem of correctly attributing malicious cyber activity is daunting. Determining who was responsible for a cyber attack is very difficult for many reasons, often including a lack of technical identification capacity. Thus, any international mechanism for collaboration and sharing of identification resources would be highly advantageous.

For this CBM, an international group of technical experts could conduct and oversee joint multinational investigations to determine proper attribution for an attack. These joint investigations will not only foster continued international collaboration on a general level (beyond the specifics of each investigation), but also serve as a deterrent to malicious cyber activity. Malicious cyber activity is often motivated by an attacker's belief that they will remain anonymous. If, however, these proposed joint investigations lead to determinations and methods of attribution, the anonymity is diminished and an attacker may reconsider their intended action.[13]

3. Promoting Collaboration and Communication of Cyber Crisis Response Teams

Given the international scope of cyberspace and cyber vulnerabilities, cyber crisis response teams must be able to quickly and securely communicate with their counterparts in other countries. Interstate and multinational mechanisms must exist for cyber crisis response teams to quickly communicate and share situational awareness. Communication must not only be between state actors, but must also include private sector entities. Basic contact lists and data sharing protocols are part of establishing this CBM.[14]

To test these communications capabilities, periodic exercises should be conducted.[15] At CHHS, we have conducted hundreds of emergency exercises for our clients. Not only do exercises provide a strong foundation to enable effective responses to real crises, but it is our experience that working through exercises establishes bonding connections among responders that serve to reinforce cooperative relationships and responses.

4. Establishment of a Norm to Restrict Certain Targets from Cyber Attack

International law establishes critical cyber targets to be focused upon for protection from attack. This proposed CBM would develop an international norm that on which parts of the cyber infrastructure need heightened protection from attack. As the Atlantic Council states, "the desired end-state of this CBM would be the acceptance of restrictions, akin to those contained in [international humanitarian law] rules, on disruptive attacks on specific assets and entities during peacetime—including but not limited to Internet backbone, major IXPs, finance, aviation, and undersea cables—that would aim to prevent the 'breaking' of the Internet." [16] International actors should collaboratively develop a common understanding of what constitutes critical cyber infrastructure and how those assets should be granted heightened protected status from malicious cyber activity.[17]

Starting on this path of CBM development, allows for a steady progression toward greater stability and security. If these CBM steps are effective and successful, others in the international community will not only adopt the norms established, but likely join in the establishment of the norms. As stated earlier, the U.S. should not wait to establish the perfect international cyber protection organization. It should quickly do what it can on an international basis and rely on successes to further develop international solutions.

No legislation needed

Finally, we believe that the recommendations we are making do not require (indeed may not lend themselves to) legislation; nor do they require anything other than de minimis appropriations. We see aggressive congressional oversight of relevant U.S. international agencies as the best method of starting and effectively implementing solutions recommended herein. As to the individual recommendations above, the Atlantic Council emphasizes, and we agree that funds for implementation would be de minimus.

End Notes

[1] CHHS is responsible for teaching "The Law and Policy of Cybersecurity" and "Cybercrimes" at the University of Maryland Francis King Carey School of Law; and it has developed cyber specializations for Masters of Science in Law (MSL) and Masters of Law (LLM) degrees.
[2] Comments made during a panel discussion at the International Conference on Cyber Engagement 2015, Georgetown University, April 27, 2015.
[3] Christopher Bronk and Dan Wallach, "Cyber Arms Control? Forget About It," March 26, 2013.
[4] The White House, International Strategy for Cyberspace: Prosperity, Security, and Openness in a Networked World, May 2011, p. 3.
[5] See Five Things to Know: The Administration's Priorities on Cybersecurity.
[6] "Federal officials call for more international cooperation in dealing with cyber crimes," Peninsula Press, February 2014.
[7] See, "Group of Governmental Experts on Developments in the Field of Information and Telecommunications in the Context of International Security," June 24, 2013.
[8] Healey J., Mallery, J., Jordan, K., and Youd N., Confidence-Building Measures in Cyberspace—A Multistakeholder Approach for Stability and Security, Atlantic Council, November 2014, [hereto forth Atlantic Council Report].
[9] Atlantic Council Report, Foreword.
[10] Atlantic Council Report, Foreword.
[11] For more information on the NIST Framework, see http://www.nist.gov/cyberframework/ndex.cfm.
[12] Atlantic Council Report, pages 4 and 16.
[13] Atlantic Council Report, p. 4.
[14] Atlantic Council Report, p. 7.
[15] Atlantic Council Report, p. 8
[16] Atlantic Council Report, p. 13.
[17] Atlantic Council Report, p. 134.

Senator GARDNER. Thank you, Mr. Greenberger.

And I will begin with my questions. In response to Mr. Painter, and in your written statement, Mr. Lewis, you stated—and I will quote—it is talking about the International Strategy for Cyber-space, the 2011 International Strategy—you said, ''That strategy now needs significant reconsideration, since we are now in a very different political environment, less peaceful, more challenging, and with overt opposition.'' You just heard Mr. Painter say that we do not really need to redo the 2011 strategy. That is our strategy. We have done a lot of—you know, had a lot of progress underneath that to fill in the buckets created by the strategy. Do you agree with him? And how would you differ? And what ought—in your opinion, ought to be done?

Mr. LEWIS. Well, I do think it was a good strategy. And I still think it lays out the basic direction that we should take. The issue is—and this gets to Professor Greenberger's remarks—we have been trying to get everyone to agree. And having sat in the room for many days with Russian and Chinese diplomats and military officials, we are not going to get them to agree anytime soon. So, is it time to take a step back and say maybe we need to agree on rules among those countries who are like-minded, among those countries who are democracies, who share values? Because I just do not think the Russians and the Chinese are that eager to agree with us on anything at the moment.

Senator GARDNER. And so, is that not—I mean, we hear about the Budapest Convention, we hear about the different working groups, and we talk about, you know, this group of people working on cyber issues here and this dialogue that is been entered there and the norms that we need to talk about. And Mr. Painter talked about norms that we have created. Mr. Greenberger talks about how we have all these groups out here that are doing these things. I mean, is it as simple as saying, ''All right, get all these groups to one big group''? I mean, what are we missing out on? Why have these norms not taken place? Because every time you read something on cybersecurity, it points to another organization that is working on cybersecurity or it was created to help deal with that. So, what are we missing, and why have not we developed, with like-minded—at least starting there—the norms that we keep talking about?

Mr. LEWIS. Well, everyone and their dog is doing cybersecurity now. And I guess that is a good thing.

Senator GARDNER. Including the Foreign Relations Committee.

Mr. LEWIS. Well, no, and I—but, your doing it is a really good thing, though. It is time for you guys to get into this business, so I am really happy to see you doing this. It is on the international security agenda. I think I said that at least twice. So, it is important that you play a guiding role in this.

With that pitch, one of the big problems is—the Budapest Convention is a classic example. This was a convention—it started out being the Council of Europe Cybercrime Convention, and the United States, Japan, Australia, a few non-European countries were also members of it. Right? And we agreed to this more than a decade ago. It is taken a while to get it endorsed by these countries. But, what you see is places like India, China, Brazil stepping back and saying, ''Hey, wait a minute. This is no longer the 1990s, where you guys can just write something and then hand it to us and say, 'Here, sign on the dotted line.' Anything we agree to, we have to participate in.'' So, there is a real fear that, if we move in a like-minded direction, we will lose the Indias and the Brazils in this world. And that is a legitimate problem. It is something that needs to be considered when we do things.

But, it has been a long time that we have been trying to negotiate these things. And I think it is worth taking a step back and saying—the proliferation example, where you did get like-minded countries together, they did agree on norms, and eventually the rest of the world adopted those norms. You know, the missile technology control regime. So, we have a fundamental decision here about, when is it time to move ahead without letting other countries have sort of a de facto veto on agreement?

Senator GARDNER. Mr. Greenberger, did you want to add to that?

Mr. GREENBERGER. Well, I am sympathetic to your concern that so many things are happening and, what impact are they having? And my measure of success is: Are we increasing the ability to stop cyber attacks? And the way you do that is to prepare both the public sector and private sector to adopt practices that make cyber attacks more difficult. That is what NIST has laid out for us. And my view would be, look, it—you can talk about 9/11 and say, What penalty should the perpetrators have paid?—et cetera, et cetera. But, what the American people really wanted is, stop those terrorist attacks. I am not saying that is the end of everything, or I am not saying that doing the Budapest Convention is not worthwhile. They are all worthwhile. But, when you are measuring—when you are starting with a massive problem, limited resources—and we have got to start measuring, Are we stopping things? The NIST protocols will stop things. There are other technical protocols that are out there that will stop things. If they do not stop things, they will identify who the perpetrators are. By the way, the five Chinese are still in China that we have indicted. We do not have them back here. We need to stop these things, and a secondary purpose is to name and shame. And, to the extent we can attribute succinctly and clearly, I believe that naming and shaming process will work.

And finally, look at NATO. NATO started out with European countries and the United States. But, the success of it caused people to want to join it. And I think that the Brazils and India and what have you, if they see somebody starting, as we said in our testimony, a single step on a 1,000-mile journey, and those single steps are effective, worthwhile, stopping attacks, people will want to come to the table. Trying to start out with a global thing of getting an agreement with everybody, I agree, is futile. We have got to start somewhere. And I would suggest these baby steps toward collaboration, norms are the way to go.

Senator GARDNER. And, Mr. Lewis—thank you, Mr. Greenberger—Mr. Lewis, just to follow up on that question. I mean, so you still think, in spite of Mr. Painter—just to get a clear answer—that a progress review of the 2011 report would be a good idea.

Mr. LEWIS. That a——

Senator GARDNER. That a progress report of the 2011 strategy would be a good start.

Mr. LEWIS. Oh, I think that would be very valuable. We have done some good things, but there are many issues that are unfinished.

Senator GARDNER. Okay. And, in my conversation with Mr. Painter, I talked about elevating the importance of cyber issues amongst our diplomatic corps. He responded with the efforts that they are undertaking. We talked about his coordination with other departments—Department of Defense, Homeland Security, and others—in their cybersecurity conversations, in their cyber conversations. Going to the structure of the cyber agencies, are we adequately communicating? How could we restructure to make sure that that—number one, the importance of the issue is elevated, but, number two, coordinating to a sufficient level and creating the kind of framework we need to respond to these kind of efforts from a diplomatic point of view?

Mr. LEWIS. Well, one of the successes of this administration has been developing a more coordinated interagency process. And so, I think Chris Painter mentioned that. I have seen that, too. If you—this is a new problem, and so the—this is only the third administration that is had to confront it, honestly. And the White House Coordinator, the White House coordination process through the NSC has been very effective.

At the Department level, there is still room for improvement. And the most obvious example of that might be DHS. DOD is making a stupendous effort to organize appropriately for cybersecurity. State did lead the way in creating a Cyber Coordinator position. It is attached to the Secretary's office.

The question now is: Do you want to embed it in the normal operations of the Department, where you have a responsible Under Secretary, a Bureau led by an Assistant Secretary, you know, an office structure below that? We have done it as kind of an ad hoc thing appended to the Secretary. Now it might be time to make that a more formal structure.

Senator GARDNER. Senator Cardin.

Senator CARDIN. Well, let me thank both of you. I find your testimony to be very, very helpful. And it does underscore the point that it is complicated. There are no simple answers.

So, Professor Greenberger, you have said our objective should be judged by preventing the bad actors from doing what they are doing. Of course, we have to define ''bad actors and what they are doing'' as being bad. But, some of this stuff is pretty obvious to us. It may not be obvious to the other side. Just pointing that out. I will get to that in one moment.

And then you said you need international collaboration. I heard you mention a couple of specifics: authenticating who is doing the business. You also mentioned developing international protocols and cooperation. But, I am not exactly sure what international collaboration would mean in stopping the bad actors. So, can you connect the dots for me a little bit better on that?

Mr. GREENBERGER. Yes. Yes. First of all, I do not think it is important to define who a bad actor is. I am reminded of Potter Stewart's famous statement——

Senator CARDIN. Yes.

Mr. GREENBERGER [continuing]. "I cannot define pornography, but I know it when I see it." And when we have these attacks, we know—we do not have to have a definition of "bad actor." We know we are in trouble, and we are angry.

In terms of collaboration—for example, in crisis management scenarios, you always have emergency operations centers communicating with each other when you have got multi-State Superstorm-Sandy kind of events. One of the recommendations of the Atlantic Council is to ensure that we have identified who the responders to the cyber crisis is in each of the countries who are like-minded with us, and that we develop a continuing working relationship with them. Another thing is to identify a priority of what infrastructures should be protected. Now, it is true, that may vary from country to country. But, there is some consensus that we can make a meaningful start in that.

Thirdly is just taking NIST and, as NIST itself has asked, internationalize their framework, or at least try to see if it can be internationalized. It is been very widely praised. There is virtually no critics to it. But, it has not been adopted elsewhere in the international sphere.

And again, I turn back to—we have hit—there is no silver bullet for this. We cannot wake up tomorrow and have the problem solved. We have got to take the first step. And the first step, to me, is gathering the like-minded together, not only nation-states, but there are very important technical institutions that are highly recognized in the United States, like the Internet Engineering Task Force, and key members, internationally, of the critical infrastructure sectors. And I believe having communications with those people, you can develop norms on how to prevent cyber attacks. You can have collaboration between countries to respond to cyber attacks. You can identify what the priorities of protection are. And, by the way, as we see in crisis management scenarios, you do not wait for a real attack; you have training, you have exercises.

I would just emphasis, Senator Cardin, as you know well, the Baltimore unfortunate situation with Freddie Gray in the last few weeks. The University of Maryland in Baltimore adopted a whole panoply of responses to ensure the safety of faculty and students. The week before the Freddie Gray event, we had an on-campus field exercise that emphasized things like shelter in place, that, a week later, were adopted in the real world. And we need to have those kinds of experiences.

The Clinton administration started with the famous "top off exercise," which I think—there were four of them. I think they hardened our domestic response to catastrophic events. We need to start thinking that way, in terms of responses to crisis events. And some of those responses are not dependent on knowing who did it. What they are responsive to is, how do we minimize the effect of an attack?

Senator CARDIN. I think that those are good suggestions. I agree that the technology at NIST needs to be better understood. Some of our frustrations in dealing—in the United States, in the private sector—is trying to get uniform technology so that we can help each other from cyber thefts. We are having difficulty in doing that.

I agree with you on having protocols on how to respond—it makes a great deal of sense.

Mr. Lewis, let me just ask—one of the challenges is that like-minded countries may differ on some strategies dealing with cybersecurity. The United States may take a pretty strong view of the need to be aggressive in stopping proliferation. Some of our like-minded countries may disagree with that type of use of the Internet and cyber in order to advance our goals. How do you reconcile homeland security issues within an aggressive use of all the tools at our disposal and still able to get like-minded protocols in place?

Mr. LEWIS. Well, one of the things that has helped us, of course—and we owe them a deep vote of thanks—is Vladimir Putin, because he has helped persuade the Europeans that maybe we are not so bad after all. So——

Senator CARDIN. I was looking for some reason to——

[Laughter.]

Mr. LEWIS. The silver lining. It is here.

It is worth noting that we cannot stop determined state actors. Right? And that is why we need international agreement, particularly the Russians, who are among the best in the world. If they want to get into your network, they are going to get into your network. And the fact that we have seen them in DOD, State, and the White House, at least at the unclassified level, is indicative of their skills. Our allies know this. And so, there are a couple levels at which we can build cooperation.

The first one, as you know, is what is sometimes referred to in the press as the "Five Eyes"—the five countries that have a very deep intelligence relationship. They are cooperating on cybersecurity. They are thinking about how to better defend themselves. The second level is NATO and our other allies, particularly Japan, Australia, Korea. These countries have begun to work closely with the United States on better cybersecurity. The European Union is an opportunity with their work in DHS. These people all share values, and they all share agreement on norms. So, while individual practices may differ—you know, France, of course, has a much more regulatory system; the Germans give a lot more attention to the privacy—but, within that, in the norm space about what responsible state behavior is, there is strong agreement among these countries, and perhaps with others. I do not mean to exclude countries like Kenya, which has been very active in this field; Brazil, which has done some good work. We have incipient partnerships that could be further strengthened, and we have existing partnerships that provide a basis for moving ahead.

Senator CARDIN. Well, let me thank both of our witnesses, Mr. Chairman. I am going to apologize, because I am being called to another committee that will be adjourning shortly, and I want to make sure I get my point in there. But, I really want to thank both of the witnesses here. I have Professor Greenberger's advice, whenever I need it, in Baltimore. And I appreciate what he does in our State. And, Mr. Lewis, I very much appreciate your contribution to this first hearing of our committee and the subject that we have.

Cybersecurity crosses many committees' jurisdictions here, and crosses many agencies in the Federal Government. And we discovered—prior to the attack on our country on September the 11th—

that we were not sharing information. And we try to take steps to correct that. I think we have come a long way, but we are not where we need to be. So, in the Congress, we need to get our act together, from the point of view of the Armed Services Committee, the Intelligence Committee, the Judiciary Committee, and the Foreign Relations Committee. I am sure there are others. And I do think that this committee can play a major role in trying to make sure that we are all coordinated in our efforts. And I thought your testimonies were particularly helpful. So, thank you both very much.

Senator GARDNER. And, Senator Cardin, thanks again for making this happen. I know you are busy, so thank you very much for participating today.

I want to continue just a few more questions as we discuss these points today. Continuing the line of thinking and the line of questioning on international norms and bringing people to the table about those norms. In your testimony, Mr. Lewis, you talked a little bit about that some people are going to fight to enter into any kind of norms, just like they did proliferation, as we have discussed. You talk about providing a mix of incentives and penalties. And so, we know the President has tools. We know the executive branch has tools now to impose certain penalties. Do you think we have gone far enough imposing, or not imposing, or should we take more of an economic sanctions kind of approach to help create the penalty phase of bringing people to the table on norms?

Mr. LEWIS. That is a great question. And I think a way to think about this—and this is very much built on the experience that began, really, in the Reagan administration and the Bush administration, on, how do you move countries like China to behave more responsibly when it comes to proliferation? And it has to be—you know, sometimes it is a push, and sometimes it is a pull. So, having done the indictments, which were very effective in China— it upset them a great deal, and that cannot always—that is probably a good thing. It certainly got their attention. Having put in place the President's ability now to sanction, with the April 1 Executive order, we need to see how our rivals react to this.

In this case, I think there is room, probably, for some negotiation with the Chinese. The Russians will be much more difficult. So, one of our—unlike the cold war, where we had there was one side, and there was the other—we have multiple potential opponents, and we may need to be different in how we react to them. It might be time for more aggressive measures, but we need to wait and see what the reaction is. Again, my measurement is really simple. Are the number of incidents going up, or down? And the answer is, they are certainly not going down.

Senator GARDNER. Mr. Greenberger, you talk about internationalizing the NIST framework and other ideas. You do not seem to talk much about punitive measures. Is that something that you could see a use for, or——

Mr. GREENBERGER. Oh, I absolutely can see a use for it. But, what I am trying to do is figure out what first steps do we need to take and get organized? You can have all the punitive measures in the world, but if you cannot identify the perpetrator, it does not help. Also, if we indict and—my colleague says that had an effect,

48

but we cannot bring them to the United States. We have got all sorts of extradition problems. I think we should move forward on all these fronts. Frankly, I think our sanctions, as we sit here now, are enough. What we need to be able to do is: (a), protect ourselves, from the attacks. And, as has been pointed out, it is not the United States protecting itself as the United States, but protecting our private infrastructure, as well. So, these are difficult things. But, my view is, the first step is, everything you read, everything you look at as a proposal, how does it give immediate relief to the problems we are seeking right now? And I think punitive damages assumes we know who the perpetrators are. And I think there is a consensus within the cybersecurity community that we may be able to say Russia or China, but we cannot say who. And if it is true that Russia and China are two-thirds, what about the other one-third who are often private citizens, hacksters who are causing all this damage? To the extent we have confidence in our ability to give attribution, many have said, and I agree, that that, in and of itself, could be a deterrence, that you cannot hide behind botnets and everything else, that you will be brought to the fore.

So, in summary, my view is that we need to look more carefully at the fundamentals. How do we prevent the attacks? How do we stop this stuff? How do we coordinate our response to attacks with other countries? How do we bring the technical expertise of the private sector to the table? That is what I think we can build on. And, as we develop that, we can identify perpetrators better, we may want to refine punitive sanctions.

And also, as to amending the 2011 Obama administration report, which we all agree was an excellent start, but if you go back and read that report, ask yourself, What steps are recommended there to prevent cyber attacks, to respond to cyber attacks, and to, as a practical matter, internationalize our response? I think, in that respect, it is 4 years ago—as you said, four centuries have gone by, in effect—but, just updating that and having more generalizations without specifics is not going to be helpful.

Senator GARDNER. Mr. Lewis.

Mr. LEWIS. Just if I could add on one point, Mr. Chairman, and thank you.

One of the significant changes in the last few years has been the ability of the United States to specifically identify the perpetrators of cyber activity. This is an effort that began probably in 2006 at the Department of Defense. And you might have seen a line in the State of the Union Address this year that hinted at how the United States does this, because the President said we would build on our experience in the counterterrorism realm of blending different sources of intelligence. So, beginning in 2006, DOD and NSA and other intelligence agencies have put a significant effort into identifying the tools that foreign opponents would use, so they could be recognized, identifying the centers that foreign opponents use, and, since Mr. Snowden has said it, I will say it, too, in penetrating foreign networks so that we can observe their activities. And putting those things together, along with human intelligence, the use of human agents, traditional signals intelligence, listening in to communications, along with cyber intelligence, has greatly improved the capabilities of the United States to specifically attribute. How this will change, I agree with Professor Greenberger, we do not know what the effect will be. But, the first time I talked to DOD about this, 8 years ago, they told me they could identify one out of three. Now I think it is well over two out of three, and maybe three out of four.

The indictments should have been a good hint to people. We have these people's pictures. I have even told some of my Chinese colleagues they have to get their hackers to dress better. We have this ability now that is not shared by other countries. One of the problems is: How do we provide that information? But, it may be worth the committee—and I know this falls a little outside of your jurisdiction, but the intelligence community has made a major effort to improve our ability to attribute attacks.

Senator GARDNER. As I learned from the House Energy and Commerce Committee, nothing is outside of our jurisdiction. [Laughter.]

The norms that we have talked about, the redlines that we have—I talked about with Mr. Painter—Mr. Painter said that there are clearly certain redlines—if somebody were to go onto a network and do some damage to a U.S. Government network or business. Do these norms need to include other redlines that—and, if so, what are they and how do we push that process?

Mr. LEWIS. In 2012, Iran began major denial-of-service attacks against leading U.S. banks. Iran, China, and Russia have probed our critical infrastructure to find vulnerabilities that could be used for a truly damaging attack, one that disrupted services or caused physical destruction; at least in the case of the Russians, they have that capability. And so, in response, then-Secretary of Defense Panetta gave a speech in New York, where he said that the United States would take action against cyber attacks that threatened to cost American lives or do significant economic harm. So, those are the two thresholds we have set. And they have been more or less reinforced since then in several statements by then-Chairman Dempsey, by Secretary Carter, by the President. There is an implicit understanding that, if people are hurt or if you do something truly significant to the economy, you face the potential for a very damaging response.

The dilemma is that everything that falls below that apparently is okay. And one of the problems we have had in this year is, we have seen both Iran and North Korea push the envelope a little bit. They did do destructive attacks against U.S. companies, against Sony and against a casino in Las Vegas. Those did destroy data, those did damage computer networks. It is a gray area, but they came a lot closer to the line. And so, one of the problems we have now is, How do we remind people, ''There are lines. Do not try and push the envelope. You need to take a step back''?

Senator GARDNER. Thank you.

And I just—to wrap this up—I do not want to keep you any longer than necessary—the final question I have is—and I know you have talked a little bit about—Mr. Greenberger, just before—Professor Greenberger—just before the last question, about what your updates to the 2011 strategic framework would look like.

Mr. Lewis, give me two or three things that we ought to start with on a progress review. And, obviously, Professor Greenberger,

I do not want to cut you off, so if you have something else that you would like to add, too, and then we will conclude.

Mr. LEWIS. We need to—as we have done in other security areas, like proliferation—assemble a group of countries that think like us, and begin to identify the norms that we think should apply, and reach agreement on them. We need to engage with the fence-sitters—India, Brazil, Turkey, the big new powers, South Africa—and keep them comfortable on this, but we do not want to give them a veto. So, I would say the most important thing we can do now is say—and as Professor Greenberger has said—get the like-minded together, get them to agree, and then get the rest of the world to go along.

Senator GARDNER. Professor Greenberger.

Mr. GREENBERGER. Yes. I agree with that. Basically, I do want to say that I am not as sanguine about our ability to identify who the perpetrators are. I think that needs to be explored. And a further point is, we do not know all the acts that have been conducted, because, as Senator Cardin said, many of the private sector do not want to identify that they have been attacked, for fear of losing the good will. So, I think that is still something to be—I think the literature, if you read it, still suggests that authentication is a serious problem.

Senator GARDNER. Yes.

Well, thank you. That concludes today's committee hearing. I want to thank the witnesses for your testimony, time, and answers today.

And, for the information of members, the record will remain open until the close of business next Tuesday, including for members to submit questions for the record. Here is the fun part. We ask the witnesses to respond as promptly as possible. Your responses will also be made a part of the record.

So, with that, thank you. Thanks, to Senator Cardin.

And this committee is adjourned.

[Whereupon, at 11:37 a.m., the hearing was adjourned.]

ADDITIONAL MATERIAL SUBMITTED FOR THE RECORD

RESPONSES OF CHRISTOPHER PAINTER TO QUESTIONS
SUBMITTED BY SENATOR BENJAMIN L. CARDIN

Question. International Standards.—As discussed at the hearing, the National Institute of Standards and Technology (NIST) has conducted cybersecurity research for decades, and leads the government in standards development and protocols for cybersecurity operations, testing, and certification. NIST's 2014 Framework for Improving Critical Infrastructure Cybersecurity references globally accepted standards and protocols, which can be used both in the U.S. and abroad to operate more efficiently and manage risks. NIST is continuing to work with foreign governments, federal agency partners, and industry stakeholders to promote the Framework and encourage alignment of compatible cybersecurity standards and practices.

♦ To what extent have these NIST standards and protocols been adopted by foreign governments? In your view, what are the major impediments for adoption of these standards? In terms of both preventing cyber attacks and identifying the source of cyber attacks, which standards should the international community adopt most quickly?

Answer. Foreign governments are well aware of the National Institute of Standards and Technology (NIST) Framework, as both U.S. officials from across the government and industry are sharing lessons learned about the Framework's development and its use throughout industry.

We believe broad use of the Framework serves as a model approach to strengthening critical infrastructure cybersecurity and that it should be adopted quickly by the international community. The aim is to promote a universally accepted and applicable approach to cybersecurity that fosters interoperability and innovation, and enables the efficient and effective use of resources.

Public-private partnerships, such as the ones being leveraged to promote the Framework, are essential to improving cybersecurity not only because the private sector owns the majority of critical infrastructure, but also because industry is most familiar with the cybersecurity products and services they develop, manufacture, deploy, and operate. As a consequence, industry is in a unique position to offer the technical and monetary resources to manage the cybersecurity risks associated with their products and services.

We have increased awareness and use of the Framework throughout the world since its launch in 2014. As two recent examples, in January, President Obama committed with the U.K. Government to "work with industry to promote and align our cybersecurity best practices and standards, to include the U.S. Cybersecurity Framework and the United Kingdom's Cyber Essentials scheme," and in April, the United States and Japan committed to "seek to enhance global resilience of critical infrastructure through the promotion of principles like those in the National Institute of Standards and Technology Framework for Improving Critical Infrastructure Cybersecurity."

I would refer any further questions regarding the NIST Framework directly to NIST.

Question. International Competitiveness for American Companies.—In the wake of the WikiLeaks disclosures, some American companies now argue they are at a competitive disadvantage when selling their cybersecurity and information technology products and services to other countries. Foreign nations have argued that U.S. companies may have to violate the privacy laws of foreign nations in order to comply with U.S. law enforcement efforts.

♦ What steps can U.S. Government agencies take in order to assuage the concerns of foreign governments that may be reluctant to purchase American cybersecurity and information technology products and services?

Answer. In a competitive ICT market, firms and service providers have an interest in providing and procuring secure, trustworthy products and services that allow customers to build resilient networks. U.S. technology companies are at the forefront of global innovation, and provide new and exciting technologies to customers around the world. Their domestic and international customers recognize and appreciate these companies' dedication to information security. In recent years, the U.S. Government, including the President, has engaged in a series of conversations and initiatives with industry to reinforce the long-standing reputation of U.S. companies as good stewards of electronic information. One example is the extensive outreach and discussions spearheaded in 2014 by then-Counselor to the President John Podesta that resulted in a detailed and comprehensive assessment and report that addressed the opportunities and challenges presented by Big Data. We also engaged industry in developing greater transparency by companies regarding government information requests. In addition, during the President's Cybersecurity Summit at Stanford University, on February 13, 2015, companies discussed key aspects of consumer protection and cybersecurity and pledged to enhance their efforts in various areas. We will continue to work with industry on these efforts.

Through our diplomatic efforts, the Department of State has worked to build trust with specific partners that have raised particular concerns, as well as with the public more broadly. For example, we addressed head-on concerns within the international Internet community in the aftermath of the initial disclosures at several high profile events, including the Stockholm Internet Forum, the Internet Governance Forum, and the Munich Security Conference. To help address concerns in Germany, in June 2014, our governments jointly organized an open, multistakeholder Cyber Dialogue hosted by German Foreign Minister Steinmeier, in which John Podesta participated, and where a high level panel of both German and U.S. experts discussed big data, privacy, security, economic innovation, and international cyber cooperation. The United States is also using every available opportunity to impress upon China our concerns regarding new draft laws and regulations that would impose restrictions on a wide range of U.S. and other foreign ICT products and services.

♦ Do these foreign governments' concerns present an additional hurdle for U.S. Government agencies attempting to promote and harmonize international cybersecurity standards? If so, what steps should U.S. Government agencies take to address and overcome these concerns?

Answer. The U.S. Government believes that using widely accepted standards helps create competitive markets around cybersecurity needs through combinations of price, quality, performance, and value to consumers. This competition then promotes faster diffusion of these technologies throughout global industry. The U.S. Government promotes policies built off those cybersecurity standards, as illustrated in the Framework for Improving Critical Infrastructure Cybersecurity developed by the National Institute of Standards and Technology (NIST). As such, we encourage foreign governments as well as partners in the private sector to evaluate these standards for themselves. We believe that this transparency serves to address many of the possible concerns foreign governments might have.

Also, as NIST continues to support and improve the Framework, it is soliciting input on options for long-term governance of the Framework including transitioning responsibility for it to a nongovernmental organization. Any transition must minimize or prevent potential disruption for organizations that are using the Framework. The ideal transition partner (or partners) would have the capacity to work closely and effectively with international organizations, in light of the importance of aligning cybersecurity standards, guidelines, and practices within the United States and globally. Transitioning to such a partner—along with NIST's continued support—would help to ensure that cybersecurity-related standards and approaches taken by the Framework avoid creating additional burdens on multinational organizations wanting to implement them.

Question. USG Interagency Coordination.—The Cyber Threat Intelligence Integration Center (CTIIC) will be a national intelligence center focused on "connecting the dots" regarding malicious foreign cyber threats to the nation and cyber incidents affecting U.S. national interests, and on providing all-source analysis of threats to U.S. policymakers. The CTIIC will also assist relevant departments and agencies in their efforts to identify, investigate, and mitigate those threats.

♦ In terms of government coordination, what do you see as the most important steps that the newly created Cyber Threat Intelligence Integration Center must take?

Answer. As noted in the background to the question, a key role for the Cyber Threat Intelligence Integration Center (CTIIC) will be to "connect the dots" regarding malicious foreign cyber threats to the United States so that relevant departments and agencies are aware of these threats in as close to real time as possible. As such, the CTIIC will provide integrated all-source analysis of foreign cyber threats and cyber incidents affecting U.S. national interests; help ensure that the U.S. Government centers responsible for cybersecurity and network defense have access to the intelligence needed to perform their missions; and facilitate and support efforts by the government to counter foreign cyber threats.

As part of these efforts, one key role that the CTIIC will take on will be to integrate and leverage the insight and information already held by the Federal Government in order to produce a more timely and holistic understanding of foreign cyber threats. In practice, relevant information from other areas of government responsibility (e.g., investigation and incident response) will be integrated with threat intelligence at CTIIC. The result should be a unified perspective that helps decisionmakers more readily understand the magnitude of a particular threat or incident and helps them ensure that appropriate actions are taken by the government. Such integration can also give federal agencies information to enhance their cybersecurity posture and can provide those federal agencies charged with supporting cybersecurity more broadly—especially incident prevention, response, and mitigation—with more timely and actionable threat information to share with their private sector partners.

I would refer you to the Office for the Director of National Intelligence for further information on the CTIIC.

———

RESPONSES OF JAMES A. LEWIS TO QUESTIONS
SUBMITTED BY SENATOR BENJAMIN L. CARDIN

Question. To what extent have these NIST standards and protocols been adopted by foreign governments? In your view, what are the major impediments for adoption of these standards? In terms of both preventing cyber attacks and identifying the source of cyber attacks, which standards should the international community adopt most quickly?

Answer. NIST has promoted its standards globally and there is interest in many countries. Some has taken the Framework as a model or as the basis for their own work. The chief obstacle to adoption is the lack of an organizational structure and authorities to implement standards. In addition to the Framework, you have ISO standards and the 20 Critical Controls as alternatives, but there is a degree of commonality among all three. The future evolution of the Framework provides and opportunity for greater engagement with foreign partners.

Question. International Competitiveness for American Companies.—In the wake of the WikiLeaks disclosures, some American companies now argue they are at a competitive disadvantage when selling their cybersecurity and information technology products and services to other countries. Foreign nations have argued that U.S. companies may have to violate the privacy laws of foreign nations in order to comply with U.S. law enforcement efforts.

♦ What steps can U.S. Government agencies take in order to assuage the concerns of foreign governments that may be reluctant to purchase American cybersecurity and information technology products and services?

Answer. Greater transparency on U.S. policy regarding IT and the relation with companies for key issues like FBI and NSA access to products and to record held by U.S. companies would help. Foreign citizens do not understand the constraints the U.S. agencies operate under, but even if they did, they might not feel more secure. The U.S. needs to accompany this with by high-level political commitments not to interfere with U.S. information technology products would help, but it will take a long time to restore confidence and success will not be easy or guaranteed. Since the effort to undermine U.S. companies is being exploited by foreign governments, the U.S. needs to take more assertive steps to counter this propaganda and expose the dishonesty of critics like Snowden and his entourage as part of a larger strategy to rebuild trust.

Question. Do these foreign governments' concerns present an additional hurdle for U.S. Government agencies attempting to promote and harmonize international cybersecurity standards? If so, what steps should U.S. Government agencies take to address and overcome these concerns?

Answer. U.S. calls for a "free and open Internet" are no longer well received by many countries in light of the NSA leaks. The entire international cyber strategy needs to take this into account and to address the concerns of key allies like Germany over data protection. The pursuit of norms and CBMs is still useful, but not enough. It's worth noting that these concerns are less those of the governments, most of whom also engage in espionage and many of whom knew of NSA activities, and more the concerns of their citizens, who will vote against politicians not seen as sufficiently assertive against the United States. The issue for NIST and other agencies is now to restore credibility and this requires more transparent and inclusive processes.

Question. USG Interagency Coordination.—The Cyber Threat Intelligence Integration Center (CTIIC) will be a national intelligence center focused on "connecting the dots" regarding malicious foreign cyber threats to the nation and cyber incidents affecting U.S. national interests, and on providing all-source analysis of threats to U.S. policymakers. The CTIIC will also assist relevant departments and agencies in their efforts to identify, investigate, and mitigate those threats.

♦ In terms of government coordination, what do you see as the most important steps that the newly created Cyber Threat Intelligence Integration Center must take?

Answer. CTIIC's job is to coordinate intelligence on cyber threats, similar to what NCTC does for terrorism. Coordination among government agencies is the responsibility of the NSC. CTIIC will need to develop the capability to acquire more than just "cyber threat" intelligence. To use Sony as an example, the first warning came from the DPRK letter to the U.N. Secretary General in the summer of 2014. This was not technical or cyber intelligence. The Center will, in additional to cyber intelligence, need to track risk in a manner similar to how large corporations track political risk. This is a significant task and to be effective, the CTIIC will need to be able to draw on the resources of the entire intelligence community.